Voices from a disused quarry:

An oral history of the
Centre for Alternative Technology

Voices from a disused quarry:
An oral history of the Centre for Alternative Technology

Allan Shepherd

©Allan Shepherd, 2015
Machynlleth, Powys
SY20 9AZ, UK
Tel. 01654 705980 • Fax. 01654 702782
pubs@cat.org.uk • www.cat.org.uk

ISBN 978-1-902175-87-4
1 2 3 4 5 6 7 8 9

The right of Allan Shepherd to be identified as the author of this work has been asserted by him in accordance with the Copyright, Designs and Patents Act 2005.

Publisher: Allan Shepherd
Editors: Catriona Toms and Rebecca Sullivan
Typesetting and cover design: Annika Faircloth
Proofreading: Rebecca Sullivan

Published by CAT Publications, CAT Charity Ltd.
Registered charity no. 265239

Voices from a disused quarry was supported by Glasu, the Society for Environmental Improvement, the estate of Gerard Morgan-Grenville and the K. Blundell Trust.

MIX
Paper from
responsible sources
FSC
www.fsc.org   FSC® C013604

Printed and bound by CPI Group (UK) Ltd, Croydon, CR0 4YY

Centre for Alternative Technology
Canolfan y Dechnoleg Amgen

Contents

Introduction

"We were all in it together. It was a great atmosphere.
I remember the chap from, I think it was *The Telegraph*
or *The Times*, came up and said this was the first real
open university he'd ever been to."

Mark Matthews[1]

A narrative history of CAT needs to be written to show the full arc of
its story, but until then, this assemblage of thematic explorations offers
the reader some direct encounters with the raw material from which
any narrative history would be written: the oral testimony of those
most directly associated with CAT – its workers, members, trustees,
friends and neighbours.

I have worked at CAT for twenty years and the dangers in writing
any history book as an insider are obvious. Being part of the story
myself it is perhaps inevitable that certain responses to the material hold
up a mirror to my own image of CAT's history rather more than they
might if an outsider had written this book. Insider insight can be both
positive and negative though, so what the reader may lose in complete
impartiality she or he will hopefully gain in colour and texture.

---

[1]   See Appendix A for more information about
     Mark Matthews and all our quoted interviewees.

To those readers who know the history of CAT intimately – being insiders yourselves – I must also offer these words: regard this book as a work in progress that can be critiqued and then adapted and expanded in subsequent editions. Due to the very practical and boring constraints of there being too little funding for a more adequate rendition, it will contain only some of the stories you would want told. Regard this first edition as the genesis for a larger work that will include more stories, a greater depth of analysis and a fuller range of voices – as soon as funding allows.

I have done my best to offer a balanced, warts-and-all account that fairly represents aspects of CAT's history. So much so that some people may think that I have dwelled not nearly enough on its successes – the achievements for which it can claim due celebration.

You will get glimpses of these successes as you read through the book but you will not find a definitive list or get a full sense of all the things CAT has done in its 40-year history. The main reason for this is that such an approach would have required an analysis of impact, and this felt like a much bigger study than anything I could achieve here. Such a project would have had to include data drawn from many more sources than the oral history interviews. Nevertheless on the timeline on pages 141–143 you will find some of the landmark moments in CAT's history. When it started, what it was trying to do, who it reached, how it evolved.

Simply reclaiming a disused quarry from idleness and putting it to work for environmental good whilst employing many thousands of people is a substantial achievement. There are other centres that have achieved similar transformations (the Eden Project and the Earth Centre for example) but CAT was the role model and did what it did with a comparatively small draw on the public purse and – compared to the Earth Centre, which closed within five years of opening – with much greater longevity.

A rough estimate suggests that around 3 million people either have visited CAT since it opened as a visitor centre in 1975, or accessed its information services, bought its books, purchased products through its mail order catalogue, and attended its short courses. 1200 students have graduated from its post-graduate courses in engineering and architecture, tens of thousands of school children have visited as part of a school group, hundreds of thousands of CAT-grown organic salads have been consumed, millions of vegetarian meals served in the restaurant, several rare species of wildlife have moved in, hundreds of six-month volunteers have received training and a way in to work, thousands of employees have had transformational experiences, and numerous life-long friendships, relationships, marriages and children have come into being.

It is impossible to measure the ripple effect of all this human interaction, nor to plot the movement of the human tides that have washed up on CAT's metaphoric shores, taken some inspiration from them and ebbed off again, carrying grains of knowledge along with them. In preparation for our 40th anniversary we received an urgent media request asking us for 40 ways in which CAT had made a difference to people's lives. We asked Facebook. Here are just a few of the many replies we received:

"Whilst working at CAT I discovered the role of education in sustainability and after having seen the inspiring work of the education department I decided to become a teacher. CAT made me realise that if you don't investigate and explore the world around you, why would you care about it, so my mission has been to make young people understand the importance of every aspect of our finite planet so they care and make positive changes that lead to sustainability. Without CAT I wouldn't be teaching in the amazing land-based school I'm currently at; it sparked my interest in self-sufficiency and farming. The Centre had a huge influence on my life and I look back with very fond memories on my summers at bottom station [working on the cliff railway]."

Victoria Hewett

"My visit as a 14 year old changed my life and made me aware of environmental issues. Now [I'm] the parliamentary candidate for the Green Party for Cotswold Constituency."

Penny Burgess

"Thanks to CAT I have changed career and started my own Eco-building business, now employing 5 others – and excited to be building our first Passivhaus."

Tim Hulse

"CAT inspired and informed our decision to build a very popular compost loo on our camp site! Kids go home and tell their teachers about how cool our tree bog is. We made new friends building it. We won a Green Snowdonia award for being a sustainable campsite. Thanks CAT."

Graig Wen

It is also undoubtedly true that without CAT many people would have been less able to express their beliefs, pursue their passions or make the kind of impact they really wanted to make, myself included. CAT has acted as an amplifier for tens of thousands of individual voices more often than not drowned out by the prevailing anti-environment 'noise'. Members and supporters interviewed for the oral history project told me that they sometimes only had the kind of conversations they really wanted to have when they came to CAT's members' conference once a year.

"I come down to most of the members' conferences, and I find it very rewarding. There are people I've met here that have influenced me and continue to influence me – well, for the rest of my life. I have done things with those people, met them at other places, gone to things that they have organised. On the basis of meeting a pair of people, engineers that I met here, I went off on a tour of Scandinavia, before devising a social enterprise which I set up in Merseyside, and put a business plan together and raised £300,000 to start that enterprise. That was entirely on the basis of the people that I've met here, and with whom I corresponded, and we continued to have a relationship outside our meeting here at a members' conference. One of the great things about it is that you meet people that you would never otherwise meet, and they talk in a language that you can understand, and that makes sense to you, in ecological terms. Whereas at home, you're often in conversations, you try to interest people, just general people, your neighbours, people you encounter through various social groups and so on, in what interests you, and they look at you askance and think, 'I don't understand that at all, and I don't want to know, thank you.'"

Judith Varley

The members, more than any other group apart from staff and trustees perhaps, have invested – both through donations and emotional commitment – a level of belief in the purpose of CAT that has sustained it throughout its 40 years. This has been particularly evident in recent years when CAT has faced its desperate hours. To give just a few examples of their largesse, CAT's supporters and members bought a million pounds' worth of shares to establish CAT PLC in the early 1990s, donated large amounts of money to help CAT buy its own site in the early 2000s, and paid for part of the construction of the Wales Institute of Sustainable Education during the mid to late 2010s. It is clear from my interviews with them that they regard this commitment as essential, so that CAT continues to deliver the meaningful and necessary change they want to see.

Chapter 1

An oral history of the Centre for Alternative Technology

Why oral history?

This book is very much the story of an oral history project. Some readers may feel that it includes a disproportionate number of words on the project itself but this is quite deliberate because I want this book to be useful to other oral historians and indeed anyone interested in setting up their own oral history project. As a first time oral historian I made quite a few mistakes organising this project but I also learned a huge amount.

The project took me in all sorts of directions I never imagined and gave me the opportunity to meet hundreds of new people, many of whom have given me fresh inspiration and even changed my life in many subtle, and sometimes dramatic, ways. I wanted to share some of this experience with you because I believe oral history projects are as much about looking after and nurturing individuals and communities in the present, and making them more resilient for the future, as they are about exploring the past.

Oral history projects allow people to come together to talk and to listen, and to explore ideas, hopes, perhaps even threats that may be common to them. They help create or strengthen networks of common purpose, providing a reflective space for interviewees as well as experiential learning opportunities for interviewers.

As an interviewer it was a great privilege to be able to ask interviewees the questions I had always wanted to ask and to really listen to them tell their stories for an hour or two. Each interview I conducted gave me access to fresh wisdom and knowledge. And when I listen back to them now I feel like I'm listening to another chapter of a favourite audio book. As a collection of voices I shall always cherish them.

The benefits of community-led oral history projects are recognised by the Heritage Lottery Fund, who have to date funded 3100 oral history projects to the tune of £81 million. I would encourage any reader to think about how they could make some of that money available to their community.

The project

The original goal of *Voices from a disused quarry* was for me to interview 20 'key' people for a book I wanted to write, and to keep these twenty interviews as an archive for future historians. But as events unfolded the project changed and grew, eventually involving over three hundred participants and reaching – through various media outlets – several hundred thousand more. In total 20 volunteers and I interviewed 100 people, creating a significant archive of over 150 hours of recorded material, which now sits in the National Library of Wales in Aberystwyth.

Furthermore:

- A separate women's oral history project called *Holdfast* has emerged, developing group interview processes through performance.

- The Arts Council of Wales has supported five artists in residence (AIR) and an AIR facilitator, who have each developed a creative response to the archive.

- The People's Collection Wales, the National Library of Wales and the University of Aberystwyth have each entered partnerships with CAT to develop and ensure public access to the archive.

- One of the project funders, Glasu, further supported a dissemination phase of the project which provided money for a new exhibition at CAT, a touring exhibition, an exhibition guide and training in oral history related performance, which led to the creation of a 'Playback Theatre' performance group and an evening performance based on the theme of *Arrivals*.

- Four project participants, including myself, created Unearthed, an oral history collective that sets out to develop projects around ecological themes. Project volunteer and Unearthed co-founder Rosie Leach, for example, is now working on an oral history project investigating flood narratives from South West England and Wales and the reflection of extreme weather in arts and performance projects.

In a way I allowed the project to show me where it could go, and this has proved its making. The depth of study and participation achieved through 'natural expansion' is a relief to me now. Choosing 'key' people would have created a bias towards a particular group identified by myself and would not have fairly reflected the self-, peer- and interviewer-identified interviewees that emerged, let alone allowing all those who participated in the project the chance not only to meet new people but to create friendships and networks that would never have existed without it.

Democratising the choice of interviewees by giving people the opportunity to *ask* to be interviewed was important to me but, despite placing bi-lingual posters in many social centres and newspaper adverts in the local press, only a handful of people asked to be interviewed, with most interviewees being 'identified' by others. The exception to this was an open request to members attending CAT's annual conference.

Before reading or listening to any of the interviews it is important to understand that the project ran at a time of great upheaval for many of the interviewees and coincided with a horrific local event that became a global news story: the abduction of 5 year old April Jones from outside her home in Machynlleth, the town at the heart of the CAT story. The interviews were recorded between 2011 and 2014, when government policy, the global recession and a legal dispute with the building contractors responsible for building CAT's Wales Institute for Sustainable Education collided to create a cash-flow crisis within the organisation, which resulted in redundancies and a substantial cut in staff hours.

It is with this backdrop in mind that the project and the voices should be considered, heard and allowed to resonate.

The oral history archive

What the National Library of Wales now holds in archive is a substantial oral history collection of interviews ranging from 30 minutes to 4 hours, not only with identified 'key' figures such as directors and long-serving members of staff, but also with numerous local people, trustees, members, 'Quarry kids', 'Quarry Wives' and staff and volunteers who were only there for a few months or years. This collection sits within a larger archive of photographs, documents, publications and videos, held by the National Library under the supervision of Michael Pearson's Mablab team.

Mick Pearson was instrumental in drawing the archive out of CAT and bringing it in to the National Library, and was the most supportive collaborator I could have hoped for in completing this project. Any reader thinking about starting their own oral history project should first think about the archiving of their interviews and find a supportive archivist who is able to work with the project. If they are anything like Mick they will help you in many ways you never expected.

For example, through Mick we worked with three post-graduate archivist students at Aberystwyth University – Kerry Evans, Ann MacDonald and Sarah Vaughan – who listened to, summarised and archived 80 interviews as part of their postgraduate studies. For this work they went on to be shortlisted for the prestigious DPC Award for the Most Distinguished Student Work in digital preservation (2014), which their supervisor Sarah Higgins tells me is the digital preservation equivalent to the Oscars. One of the students, Sarah Vaughan, went on to work at CAT and another, Ann MacDonald, got her first job in digital preservation at the British Library.

Mick also worked with me to create an archive launch event at the National Library, which brought together 10 speakers, each giving 10-minute talks, as well as a *Holdfast* collective interview, an exhibition, a performance of a 40th anniversary song by folk singer and CAT employee Rebecca Sullivan, and the launch of a new social sculpture by artists in residence Christine Mills and Carlos Pinatti entitled *Receive and Return*. The launch event itself brought more people into the project, including the National Library's Head Librarian and Chief Executive Aled Jones, who signed the deposit agreement with me on the steps of the National Library, one of the proudest moments of my life.

Taking the archive to the National Library of Wales – the repository and protector of the nation's cultural life – felt like a big deal. We wanted to do something special to celebrate it, and also celebrate the journey CAT has taken. So we decided to take a journey of our own: on the morning of the archive launch event ten of us each carried a piece of the archive along a six mile stretch of coastline path between Borth and Aberystwyth, climbing the hill to the National Library in our shorts on a hot summer's day before donning our smart clothes and presenting the archive.

'Journeying the archive' allowed us to share conversations about the past and the future whilst celebrating the landscape of the Dyfi Valley. Also we got to see firsthand the building of coastal sea defences in storm-ravaged Borth, a hint of the scale of adaptation that will be required as climate change takes hold. Along the way we recorded interviews about the archive pieces we were carrying and what they meant to us. Here, three people not 'captured' during the main oral history project share their thoughts on the objects they carried.

"*Zero Carbon Britain: Rethinking the Future* is the report published from 2013. I'm taking this to the National Library because this is a piece of the recent history and the output of CAT. It's a report that we wrote that explains how the whole of the UK could be powered on renewable energy without greenhouse gas emissions. The part I'm specifically going to read is about how we deal with the fact that the wind sometimes blows and sometimes doesn't, and the sun sometimes shines and sometimes it doesn't, and some people think that's a reason for not having renewables, but we think otherwise."

Tobi Kellner

"I've got a booklet called *Activities for Children*. I chose it because some of the activities in here I remember doing in 2001 at a Woodcraft Folk camp, and a group of people from CAT came and ran a kind of centre there, and I remember making some of these solar cookers and a bike trailer there. I think it was that camp that really made me think of doing environmental science at University. So this activity book has had quite an impact on my life."

Kit Jones

"This is the first issue of *Clean Slate*, which replaced the original Quarry News, which was a newsletter put out for the members. The editor was Dilwyn Jenkins at that time. Winter 1989. I'm taking this to the library because I'm part of the membership team and membership has been such an important part of CAT since the beginning. I like the original layout. Nice and nitty gritty and down to earth."

Rebecca Sullivan

The interviews

"We had 80,000 customers. The big year, we put 800,000 flyers in various magazines. It was big. A big thing to be part of. We held a huge amount of stock here, for an 80-page catalogue that had six things on every page. Because trade has contracted now I look around and think: how did we do it in this room? There were 9 people working in it. We were the first retailer of environmental products and books. The catalogue was called *Buy Green by Mail* and that was a claim we could make: we were the people who you bought green things from by mail. We were a big income generator for the company. It felt important what we were doing. It felt necessary. It was what customers wanted and it was a very significant thing for CAT for us to be making that income. I remember this amazing sense that I was working hard for a reason, a collective endeavour. A big extension of what CAT was doing. Just knowing that you were part of a large network and quite a big movement."

Bethan Bennett

We did our best to represent all work areas at CAT in the oral history project so we have interviews with educators, engineers, biologists, builders, architects, gardeners, designers, publishers and administrators; as well as retail, restaurant, finance, media, membership, maintenance, visitor centre and fundraising staff.

We also made sure we interviewed people from each of CAT's four decades, generating strings of interviews in many work areas that carry right through from the early 70s to the present day. This approach has given us valuable information about the development of environmental technologies and ideas, as well as changes in, for example, design standards, not to mention responses to developments in mainstream technological and political change – for example the arrival of computerisation and the internet, or Welsh devolution.

Some work areas have been more fully captured than others. For example, we were able to interview education officers who had served from 1977 on, including, in chronological order: Nigel Dudley, Joan Randle, Damian Randle, Ann MacGarry, Christine McLennan,

Jo Gwillim and Julie Bromilow. Anyone interested in environmental education can follow the interviews through and get a detailed picture of the development of techniques and ideas from the mid 1970s to the present day. For example, here Julie Bromilow explains some of the complexities associated with delivering sustainability workshops to hundreds of school groups in the early 2010s.

"Tutors definitely need a lot of hand holding when it comes to sustainability, that's why we were working with education advisors and exam boards as well, and also to provide teacher and tutor training to try and make sure the tutors and teachers felt confident in teaching sustainability themselves. The main problem with that is that they have a short amount of training, some of it several years ago, and they don't feel confident in keeping up with something which is fast paced, changing; they're not on top of the issues. They've only typically received an hour's training on sustainability within their whole teaching training experience. They quite often don't feel confident in it and rely on the education office at CAT to provide the whole of the sustainability experience, which of course is a massive challenge, because it's a huge, huge topic. Sometimes we'd only get half an hour with [a group] (laughs) and you'd have to try and provide a really positive experience that they're going to enjoy, and feel confident in addressing sustainability issues through practical action, but also dispelling some of the myths as well; while at the same time making sure that you weren't providing a didactic experience. So we always tried to make sure that we were giving them enough information to make their own choices, but that they were confident in doing that without feeling that they'd been told what to do, and also that they felt confident in asking as many questions as they felt necessary. So it was quite a challenge to pack so much into a small amount of time, but that was why we were really concerned with working within the broader education sector as well, in particular with trainee teachers and within the sector as a whole, rather than just providing nice experiences for pupils to have on a day out."

Julie Bromilow

See Appendix B for photo captions

The collection also contains interviews with each of CAT's directors, except Mary Mathews, who we have been unable to capture so far. In chronological order these are: Mark Mathews, Rod James, Pete Raine, Roger Kelly and Paul Allen. These interviews tend to focus more on institutional and management change but also give an overall impression of how CAT changed from one leadership era to the next. Interestingly CAT also had periods without a director, between Pete Raine and Roger Kelly, and between Paul Allen and the appointment of CEOs Elfyn Jones and Adrian Ramsay in 2012 and 2014 respectively, neither of whom has as yet been interviewed. Peter Harper talks a little about these 'interregnums' in his interview.

After Roger Kelly left, a new role of administrative director was created – filled by Liz Doyle (not yet interviewed) and Eileen Kinsman (interviewed) – and the director role became more external facing. This role was also discontinued. It should also be noted that CAT also elected PLC directors from the staff body (some of whom have been interviewed and are listed in the oral history archive).

If you are particularly interested in CAT's management structures, listen to all these interviews alongside those of trustees Delyth Rees, Cynog Dafis, Iolo ap Gwynn, Liz Todd, Jill Whitehead and Martin Ashby, as well as company secretary Rick Dance (please note that the first three interviews in this list are conducted in Welsh, and English transcripts are available).

The oral history archive catalogue (available from http://archive.cat.org.uk) groups interviews into ten work areas – senior management (see above), biology, engineering, architecture and construction, site maintenance, visitor services, education, communications, finance (donors and fundraising), administration – and two non work-related themed groupings: Dyfi Valley community, history and association.

The catalogue is incredibly useful when people are only employed in one work area and a little less useful if a person has had several jobs at CAT in very different areas. For example my archive colleague Peter Harper has worked as landscape co-ordinator, visitor centre displays co-ordinator, biologist, head of research and innovation, Zero Carbon Britain land use researcher and archive project co-ordinator. Furthermore he is also well known as the person who coined the phrase 'alternative technology' and as the lead researcher of the team responsible for developing the cool composting technique, widely adopted throughout Britain. But his interview is also interesting because it contains lots of valuable thoughts on the development of science and on how science relates to environmentalism and, more specifically, to the evolution of CAT's philosophy.

Listening to interviews in full is the only way to really know them but the archive catalogue also has short summaries of each interview to act as a guide. As well as searching through work areas you can search for key words; the inquisitive researcher will thus be able to find links between disparate interviews in seemingly unrelated areas. Peter Harper's digital image project *Re-storying the Archive* (not yet archived) takes this one step further by adding comments to archived digital photographs, allowing researchers to search between different media using key words. We are currently waiting for further funding to complete this work and make it available.

Thus, using the oral history catalogue, it is possible, for example, to search for references to the Wales Institute of Sustainable Education, CAT's most significant architectural achievement to date, and find interviews with architects Pat Borer and David Lea, project manager Phil Horton and other people at CAT who played a part in its development, including CAT's former builder Cindy Harris, fundraisers Rachel Lilley, James Cass and Tanya Hawkes, and Graduate School founder Joan Randle, not to mention trustees, members and donors.

Interviews can then be listened to in clusters and the links drawn between them. For example, the four-hour interview with WISE Architect Pat Borer covers the whole history of building and architecture at CAT, but his interview should also be listened to alongside those of second director and architect Rod James, fourth director and architect Roger Kelly, long-time CAT builder Cindy Harris, and CAT associate architects David Lea and Patrick Hannay. Taken as a whole, this cluster of interviews provides an insightful account of the evolution of environmental building philosophies, techniques and materials at CAT that, in turn, tell you a lot about CAT's thinking and practical concerns at particular times in its history. Let's run with the architecture story a little to get a sense of what I mean.

Architectural development stories at CAT

Here are the two Patricks – Hannay and Borer – talking about CAT's first modern architectural statement, the Autonomous Environmental Information Centre (AtEIC), designed by Pat Borer and David Lea and opened in 2000. Before AtEIC most of CAT's buildings were constructed or re-built following a vernacular architecture tradition or using simple self build models. This often led to criticism of CAT's design standards and aspirations, giving people the opportunity to dismiss environmentalism as being somehow anti-modern and anti-design. On the other hand many people felt empowered by the simple un-fussy, unglamorous self build approaches CAT taught.

Nevertheless AtEIC showed that an environmental philosophy could deliver progressive, beautiful and light spaces. As well as incorporating environmental technologies such as rammed earth walls and passive solar gain, AtEIC also featured the construction of a new district heating system, which allowed renewable heat energy to be moved around site.

"I was very aware that one of CAT's great bibles [was] *Architecture without Architects*. It's a very radical book and it's all about self build and collaboration and people just coming together and building something out of any local material resource they could find, and you didn't have architects anywhere near it. So there was this notion that only grew up very strongly in Britain that actually the environmental movement was sort of separate from good architecture. The underlying implicit message from the environmental movement was 'We don't need you, this is not to do with you', or 'Don't you try and make us design this really elegantly because that's not what this is.' I began to go 'round CAT [in the early eighties] thinking 'God this is really tatty, these graphics are dreadful, the way this whole place exudes a make do and mend …', and if you're wanting to inspire students that environmentalism and elegant beautiful architecture are all one, then CAT as a leading promoter of environmentalism in architecture needed to really up their game. Students saw it as quaint or separate but they didn't go there and say 'Oh wow, that piece of architecture is amazing.' As AtEIC started to come that was better and the students began to realise that elegant architecture and environmentalism was all one."

Patrick Hannay

"The railway station is a very traditional looking building but we felt that these [older] buildings were not appealing to the modern architectural world so [AtEIC] was the first building where we thought that we would make this a piece of modern architecture – lots of daylight, a wall of glass, a wall of solid, very clean lines, simple repetitive roof structure. What architecture gives you is space, that quality of light and volume that we call architecture. And I think it's got it, it's got a presence as you go into the shop. It's 'Whoa, this is good.' You could have made it much more utilitarian, it would have worked just as well, but it wouldn't have that certain something to sell the idea of green construction. Gerard [Morgan-Grenville] called it 'a cathedral of green construction.'"

Pat Borer

In many ways the construction of AtEIC was a turning point for CAT, as it showed that CAT could be entrusted with large amounts of public funding to deliver something modern and relevant that could change the way people viewed environmental architecture. It had the backing of many prominent people in Wales and represented a leap towards putting environmental thinking into the mainstream. It enabled the provision of free information services to hundreds of thousands of people and the blossoming of CAT's mail order business, as described by Bethan Bennett in her quote on page 13. It also led indirectly to the construction of the Wales Institute for Sustainable Education and the creation of CAT's Graduate School of the Environment.

The Graduate School of the Environment and WISE brought hundreds of students and a previously unknown level of mainstream educational and architectural respectability to CAT. The graduate school set up its own Professional Diploma in Architecture and the WISE building made the long list for the prestigious Stirling Award as well as winning several other awards.

See Appendix B for photo captions

"What we always wanted to do was to show people that you could have comfort and warmth and light in a building which had low impact, and that wasn't the case in our other buildings. What we want to show people is what we know, that you can build sustainable low-impact buildings. And we want people to learn in that kind of building and not learn and suffer in a building that's cold and not properly insulated. There are so many graduates gone from CAT in the last 12 years who are in influential positions in the UK and throughout the world relating to sustainability, and that's what we're supposed to be [at CAT] for."

Joan Randle

"There was always talk that it was going to become a university, right back at the beginning. That was always the thing. It's taken 35 years to do it. But it's a very exciting moment that – the [formation of the] Graduate School."

Rod James

Re-storying the archive

There was a sense of urgency about capturing the voices of those people who lived and worked at CAT in the 1970s. To this end Archive Project Coordinator Peter Harper set about digitising and 're-storying' thousands of images, inviting early pioneers to record the details of the people, technologies and activities shown in each photo (an example of which can be found here).

Elektro 5 kW machine damaged by lightning
Andy Brown
Guy Watson
"Looks like a crashed aeroplane"
Bob Todd took a blade to a talk at BWEA[1] meeting in London, on the tube!
Broken blade visible

---

[1]   British Wind Energy Association

Thanks to some good advice from one of our funders – Powys-based organisation Glasu – we booked a training day with Julia Letts of the Oral History Society at the start of the project. As a novice oral historian this turned out to be the best advice I received early on in the project. I do, however, wish I had received it before applying for funding, as Julia's suggestion to allow 10 hours for each interview to be researched, completed, backed up and documented would have been very useful. As it was, we had an over-ambitious target of 80 interviews to gather in far less time than we really needed.

Together with Julia we set down a list of key historical 'themes' in a rough schematic that would form the template for how each interview would be conducted. Rather than ask each interviewee a set list of questions we would explore themes within their own personal histories and the history of CAT. This would allow the interviews to remain free but focussed.

At first these themes were pretty sprawling but during the project I boiled them down to the following four: Environmental Quest, Technical Endeavour, Sense of Place, and Community and Co-operation. This last theme later became Community, Conflict and Co-operation, on the suggestion of one of the volunteers, who thought I was missing a vital part of the history – as well as being too positive!

Briefly, Environmental Quest is CAT's journey towards defining what it believes in; Technical Endeavour represents the struggle to develop better alternative technologies; Sense of Place asks how CAT's location affected its history; Community, Conflict and Co-operation looks at the unique co-operative management structure and on-site community. Most of the rest of the book is based around explorations of these emergent themes.

Within each of these themes we identified 'areas of interest', for example 'communal lunches', 'the Welsh language', 'class dynamics', 'volunteering', 'on-site accommodation', 'equal pay' and 'on-site farm animals'. Then within these areas of interest we noted the nomenclature or 'key words and phrases' defining specific places, activities or objects, such as: Tea-Chest, the pig debate, all-staff meetings, the old quarry, the Cretan windmill and so on. During our training day with Julia Letts we took our volunteers through each of these themes, areas of interest and key words and phrases.

It was almost impossible to keep all of this in mind when conducting an interview but it was possible to remember many of the key words, some of the areas of interest and all of the themes. This allowed the interviewer to build up a set of questions in their mind and keep the interview moving whilst allowing interviewees to say what they wanted to. In addition we asked each interviewee to say their name and what their connection to CAT was, when they were at CAT and what their life would have been like if CAT had never existed.

I called this my *'It's a Wonderful Life'* question, after the 1947 black and white movie starring Jimmy Stewart in which Jimmy's character George Bailey gets the chance to see what the lives of his family, friends and community would have been like if he had never been born – and in the process to learn how important he is to all of them.

In the interviews no one had time to prepare for the *It's a Wonderful Life* question and the answers were quite often spontaneous and heartfelt. Not everyone reveals a life-changing experience. It's true that some answers are not at all long, and some people can't see that CAT has made that much difference to them at all.

But on the whole the answers revealed that CAT gave people a sense of deep connection to ideas, life experiences and other people.

"I could point to other things that I have learnt [from CAT] like the ins and outs of climate change policy or how to get more hits on Facebook, or how to drive traffic to your blog, but all of that I can guarantee you is going to be irrelevant in fifty years, whereas learning how to negotiate compromise, interact with people, respect people, respect people's opinions, listen to them, understand what they need from you, why they're worried about what you're planning to do, explain what you're thinking clearly to someone else, it's not going to go out of date really, I don't think, so that's the thing that I take away from CAT really, is having learnt to do that."

Alex Randall

We captured as much detail as possible about choices related to work, including technologies developed, dates, how decisions were made, why a particular technology or idea failed under testing or was abandoned for other reasons. The idea of 'allowable failure' became another area of interest, which I cover in greater detail on pages 103–105. We also wanted to know why people left CAT, what they went on to do after they left and whether CAT had changed them.

We asked questions about childhood, education and background to try and get a sense of what influenced interviewees and why they became involved with CAT. We wanted to know how an environmental consciousness emerged and what it was like to be an environmentalist during this period of rapid environmental change. At the end of each interview we asked interviewees if there was anything they wanted to add.

"The thing we haven't really touched on is what motivates people to do environmental work and I think I'd want to recognise the fact that people put so much heart and soul into it and suffer so much angst for what they believe in. Because CAT is a fantastic place, and there's loads of ups and downs and all that, but generally we are a group of people who try and do our best, and there's some lovely people there, and we have some great times, but also people really, really suffer for trying to do something about what they believe in. And I think for anyone working for something that they really believe in, and are scared of negative outcomes, people care is really important, and in the environmental movement I'd like to see more attention given to mental health issues, because it's really hard when you're working because, say, you're scared of climate change, and perhaps you don't feel like you're getting anywhere. I think that can be really hard and I think it's something that we don't talk about that much."

Chloe Ward

Areas of interest: some examples

There are many areas of interest waiting inside the archive for the curious observer: 'financial structures', 'fundraising', 'the gardens', 'biological services', 'CAT's ecology', 'volunteering', 'growing up at CAT', but here are a few that cropped up in a substantial number of interviews.

Low and flat: wages at CAT

Most people interviewed showed themselves to hold ideals that were, and still are, very much at odds with mainstream consumer capitalist values. Phrases similar to 'Nobody ever came to CAT to get rich' came up in one form or another many times over during the interviews and a great deal of pride was held in such statements. Some people might have found it hard to 'go without', but they did so nevertheless with unwavering belief that it was the right thing to do.

When in the UK, as a whole, pay differentials between the lowest paid worker and highest paid manager in organisations rose, at CAT they stayed the same. Up until 2012 the differential had never been more than about 1.3:1. Even now it is approximately only 3:1. This is highly unusual, even for a charity, and more so for society as a whole. In 2014 a FTSE 100 Chief Executive earned on average 120 times more than a full time employee – in 2000 that figure was just 47 times. (Research by Income Data Services quoted in *The Independent* on 14ᵗʰ October 2014).

> "I don't think anyone suffered but we didn't have spare money. There are lots of people who earn low wages and there are billions of people around the world who don't have enough to eat, that's a different thing, but we were all professionals and we chose this. We could have been paid a lot more but we chose to do this because that's what we wanted to do. I'd like to think that 30 years wasn't wasted, so I obviously will think that putting all that time and effort into working at CAT did produce some beneficial results, and I do think that's true."
>
> *Joan Randle*

"People don't come here because it's convenient or accessible or because they can make loads of money here, even because of university or jobs. It's this delicate balance of factors that seems to have created the most lovely community for me to grow up in. I really wasn't aware that was so special when I was young. It was a revelation to realise it wasn't the case the world over."

Megan Mills

CAT has experimented with several different flat (ish) pay structures over the years. In the 1970s and 1980s a basic equal wage was supplemented with needs-based payments for children and discretionary payments that fell under schemes with names like 'Banana stopper' (to stop you going bananas).

"Bob [Todd] and I assessed what everyone should be paid. We sort of worked out what people were worth. If they were living off site they needed more than if they were on site. If they had a child they needed more money than someone who didn't have any children. You had to work through all those things. Bob and I came up with these figures, and everyone said you've got no right to do that. So we said, 'Fine then, you do it. You all be part of it then.' So we produced this sort of list of ten points, qualities. There was one you got paid for being, one you got paid for what you were doing, whether you had particular skills, whether you introduced something that was just fantastic, you made people laugh or you made people nice food, and we got everyone to assess everyone else in the group, everyone, and themselves. It was very interesting. One person valued herself as the bottom and everyone else valued her as being extremely good. And one person valued themselves as being extremely good and were valued by everyone else as being extremely poor. Apart from that, in the 25 people, the rest were exactly the same as Bob and my intuitive response."

Rod James

Later on – in the mid to late 80s – casual and associate co-op member rates were introduced for staff who were considered to have less responsibility or permanence than full co-op members. This system more or less stayed the same till 2012, but with the addition from 2007 onwards of academic pay scales.

Phrase mythology at CAT

I have worked at CAT for twenty years so I was also already familiar with the mythology of the organisation: the stories – sometimes simply expressed as phrases – we shared amongst ourselves, those we shared with the outside world and those the outside world used to describe us.

Can we assume that myths – as opposed to lies – hold some degree of truth? In any case it is important to unravel them because they can also hold back real understanding and consequently real change.

At CAT we used myths to tell our story to the world, to define perceived progress amongst ourselves as we developed and – through the telling of 'inheritance stories' – to maintain group purpose and unity. People outside of CAT also created their own myths about CAT to define what they thought about us, to reinforce their own world-views and to create their own group cohesion as a reaction to our presence.

'Phrase mythology at CAT' and 'inheritance stories' thus became areas of interest. Phrases such as 'crazy idealists', 'workers co-op', 'village of the future', 'off-the-grid', 'living laboratory', 'Europe's leading eco-centre' are part of the cultural fabric of the place and came up in many interviews, as did the words 'pioneers', 'amateurs' and 'hippies', used to describe CAT staff.

The role of class at CAT, Gerard Morgan-Grenville and Diana Brass

Another area of interest is 'the role of class at CAT'. CAT was founded by the grandson of the last Duke of Buckingham and Chandos, Gerard Morgan-Grenville, a charming and straight-dressing member of the aristocracy with a background in entrepreneurial business and an interest in environmental alternatives. Returning from a trip to the United States in 1973, where, along with fellow environmentalist Diana Brass, he had visited a number of communities experimenting with alternative technologies and lifestyles, he was determined to set up something similar in Britain.

Unfortunately I didn't have the chance to interview Gerard, as he died in 2009, but he left behind many broadcast interviews and his autobiography *Breaking Free*.

"With a fierce concentration, I focused on one central idea, the setting up of this centre where people, ordinary passers-by, might readily perceive the disastrous course on which our civilisation was set and be shown things they, anyone, might do to reduce their impact on the environment. Ways of life which the planet could sustain were to be suggested and some of the more obvious methods of achieving these would be demonstrated. It was intended to show a range of practices which would have minimal adverse consequences both environmentally and socially. It was also proposed that books and pamphlets would be available for sale, and finally that, both in order to put these ideas to the test and to gain public credibility, those who lived and worked there would be as self-reliant as possible."

Gerard Morgan-Grenville (from Breaking Free)

From the point of view of the oral history project it was obvious from the start that Gerard was going to be an 'area of interest', as was his co-founder Diana Brass. The relationship between them, their personalities and their roles within the organisation are central to CAT's foundation and early survival. But so too is their position of influence within society and what that meant for the development of CAT and of the environmental movement more generally.

"I think he was someone who was possessed with a mind that was extraordinarily prescient. Looking back to the early 70s it must have been a hard task to try and anticipate what the energy issues were going to be 30 or 40 years hence. However he was the type of person who, when he got the bit between his teeth, the more sedulous side of his nature would kick in, and he would fight for whatever it was he wanted to achieve until he achieved it. He was very, very determined."

George Morgan-Grenville

"[Diana] was absolutely astonishing. She would work bashing up slate and making paths and planting gardens and everything else, and cooking for an unlimited number of people who went through there. Just astonishing."

Rod James

There is no doubt that Diana Brass' unyielding dedication to 'the Cause', her passion for CAT and determination to live simply in very difficult conditions, combined with Gerard's charm, influence and ability to secure donations, pulled CAT through many dark days. Whilst Diana dug paths and cooked meals with limited food supplies for endless volunteers, Gerard sold CAT's principles and activities to supporters, recruited staff and used his status to make sure CAT's mission was understood and respected.

For example, when *The Times* refused to accept an ad from CAT politely asking if any of its readers had "a month to spare" – on the grounds that CAT was an anarchist organisation – it was left to Gerard to make a phone call to put the matter straight. The ad ran, and was extremely successful in recruiting volunteers, amongst them Richard St George and Des Rees – incidentally both from very different backgrounds – who became very good friends.

"I originally got to know about the Quarry when I was looking to do a trip, out in the Sahara, joining someone in a Landrover, cos I happened to have some money at that time. The only thing I saw that seemed vaguely interesting was this little advert 'have you a month to spare' in the Personnel column of *The Times*. 'Have you a month to spare – some building experience will be a help', I think that was it, and to be honest, I didn't have a huge amount of building experience at that

time cos I'd come up from a farming background actually and
had since worked in the city, up in Sheffield in a John Lewis
Partnership shop, so I had a sort of very varied background at
that point. Had absolutely no idea what alternative technology
was about, but it just sounded, well, it was better than
nothing."

Des Rees

Early patrons and supporters

The notion that CAT was an anarchist organisation is difficult to
substantiate when you take a closer look at lists of early benefactors,
patrons and consultants, which included six professors, three lords,
three sirs, three people in receipt of other royal honours and an Earl –
all pillars of the British establishment.

Patrons
Lord Annan, OBE, MP
Rt. Hon. Roy Jenkins, MP
Rt. Hon. Lord Robens of Woldingham
Sir Bernard Waley-Cohen

Early 'Industrial and commercial donors of materials and equipment'
This is just a small selection of the 101 industrial companies
named as donors in a visitor guidebook from the early 1970s.

*Acrow, Associated Portland Cement, Black and Decker Ltd, Bovis Ltd,
British Industrial Plastics, British Rail, Chloride Industrial Batteries,
Chubb Fire Security, Cuprinol Ltd, Dawes Bicycles, Dexam International,
Easyfix Double Glazing Ltd, General Electric Co Ltd, ICI Ltd, Laura Ashley,
Lockhart Service Depot, National Coal Board, Pilkington, Rentokil,
Sir Robert McAlpine, Spear & Jackson, Taylor Woodrow Construction,
Wates Built Homes.*

The visitor centre

CAT's visitor centre was opened in 1975, and it's difficult to imagine what CAT would be without it. At its peak in the early 1990s, just after the cliff railway was built, it attracted over 90,000 visitors a year.

Almost every interview contains a reference to the visitor centre, and most of those people who do mention it have strong feelings about it. The visitor centre was the glue that bound most departments together because most departments either serviced the visitor centre or were dependent on it in one way or another.

> "[The purpose of the education department is] to provide high quality education about sustainability for school groups and teachers through the day visits and the [eco]cabins. In order to do that, we need to have an input into displays. We're very lucky. I think we have the best jobs at CAT because we get the feedback. We get to interact with all these people and get feedback from them and get a buzz out of that – in doing these things successfully. We interact with the site with more people than anybody else does and with a bigger variety – because we have also done adult groups and university groups [as well as school groups]. We learn how difficult to understand some [of the displays] may be, and we discover the things that make them [the children] laugh and provide an opportunity to put over a message that sticks. We still mourn the loss of things like the bottle dome; it was just fun. The big old wave machine we had, that was brilliant. Water went everywhere. If they could splash their teachers, great; teachers didn't mind."
>
> *Ann MacGarry*

Particularly before the internet, the visitor centre was the way many people first encountered CAT. During a visit they might find out about short courses, membership, publications, mail order, the eco-cabins, the information service and so on. For some interviewees a visit to CAT's visitor centre as a child was the trigger for a career at CAT later on; remembering their visit, in adult life they returned as volunteers or staff members.

Village of the future?

See Appendix B for photo captions

"How I first came across CAT was that we had a family holiday in Barmouth when I was twelve years old. And I don't remember very much about CAT but I remember one particular display, and I suppose I just knew that CAT existed and it seemed a really good place to spend six months as a volunteer whilst I worked out what I wanted to do after finishing my thesis. And I don't suppose I ever decided what I did want to do, and I was at CAT for the best part of twelve years, all in all."

Judith Thornton

In the early days admittance to the visitor centre was very informal. In his interview George Morgan-Grenville relates a story of a boyhood stay with his father at the Quarry, where one of his jobs was to stand at the top of the drive with a tub collecting the 50p entrance fee. The display circuit was also very informal. Rough paths around the site had been hewn from the slate, and primitive displays could be found in various corners. An exhibition was erected in the old machine room. Over a five-year period between 1975 and 1980 gardens, smallholding, a shop and restaurant were added, as well as more sophisticated displays and energy experiments.

Although some people were undoubtedly put off by the visitor centre's (by some standards) shabby appearance, it attracted between 40 and 60,000 people annually through most of the 70s and 80s. Second director Rod James believes people came because it was a fun place to visit. The issues were serious but the place itself was fun, and people could see what CAT was trying to achieve. Display boards had very few words, graphics and cartoons being preferred (listen to the interviews of Pat Borer, John Urry, Peter Harper and Graham Preston for further insights).

By the late 80s, however, visitor expectations were changing, and it became clear that if CAT was to reach out to a wider audience it would have to re-design the visitor experience. It did this by building a water-balanced cliff railway to take visitors from the car park to the main site and by re-landscaping the entrance around a new lake that would hold the water needed to lift carriage loads of people from the bottom to the top station. The old railway track that had been laid in 1974 and 75 was also removed to enable better visitor access around site. The changes worked, raising visitor numbers from approximately 60 to 90 thousand a year, although it should be noted that this fell far short of the hoped for target of 150,000. There were no further substantial changes to the visitor centre until Peter and Carrie Canham (not yet interviewed) created the Bringing the Future Forward project in 2006.

Unlike some departments where staff turnover has been quite low, the visitor centre has had quite a high turnover of staff. Because of this it has been impossible to interview visitor centre co-ordinators in a continual line, although Peter Harper and Andy Rowland both played central visitor centre roles. There is also a detailed account of the history and mechanics of the cliff railway in Chris Parrot's interview. Chris has records of cliff railway journeys stretching back throughout its lifespan. Here he recalls the cliff railway's busiest afternoon, as expressed by the number of trips the cliff railway made, and compares it to journeys made on the day of his interview in October 2012.

"16th August 2000 was the busiest afternoon, with 103 trips, and the following morning were 62 runs, and those were figures that were perhaps slightly above what was a normal day's work at that period. [My abiding memory?] I think it will be the way we worked in those extremely busy days and we had to have very good teamwork between top and bottom stations to eke out the water. When the lake level was low we had to cut back the number of people that we could haul up. And there was great teamwork, so that the moment we had visitors going down we could increase the number we could bring up on a trip. If you could increase the up-haul by five people a trip, three trips was fifteen people, and that was equivalent to another trip. And this was very important. At that period it was not unusual to have a queue from the reception desk, all the way down the ramp and right across the car park, possibly a half hour queue time."

Chris Parrott

Poo

At some point – nobody knows when, somebody – nobody knows whom – christened CAT 'the shit and wind'. Whoever and whenever it was, the phrase stuck, at least locally. Many of us who have worked up at CAT have had it said to us in one way or another over the years: 'Still working up at the shit and wind?'

As shit and wind – not to mention urine – have been common areas of interest throughout CAT's history, the acquisition of such a nickname is hardly surprising. Indeed most people who have come to work at CAT have developed a healthy interest in both. Inductions would invariably include a tour of the windmills (which I go on to talk about on pages 105–109) but also of the wide range of alternative toilets available to use, from the ornately spired but ultimately utilitarian 'pee chest', to the des res, worm composting loo that was funded by the Bill Gates Foundation.

Interest in all things scatological was celebrated in one of CAT's books from the 1990s, *Lifting the Lid.* Written by Peter Harper and Louise Halestrap, *Lifting the Lid* had the working title *Taking the Piss and Winning the Poo* and contained, along with all the collective wisdom of twenty years of compost toilet experimentation, a list of alternative titles thought up along the way. Amongst other things the book introduced readers to phrases such as 'peak knocker'.

All of our 'biological' interviewees – in chronological order Jeremy Light, Peter Harper, Louise Halestrap and Judith Thornton – talk with great affection of their adventures in sewage. In her interview below, Lousie Halestrap describes a typical round of toilet duties, here taking in the reed bed sewage system and the compost toilets.

"It's lovely. It's like a wetland. That's what it is, a constructed wetland. You've got phragmites reeds growing there, bullrushes and other reed plants, and then you have reed buntings and all sorts of rare little birdies. It's a very nice place to be. There's a little bit of a smell from the septic tank but it's not atrocious, but it's the most loveliest system. And it's all gravity fed, so once you've put the embodied energy in, in the liner and the stones and things, it's just left. There's some clever little gizmos that are using no electricity and no moving parts that allow the water to flow either on the left hand one or the right hand one and pulsate the flow. It was a very nice place to work. We used to walk down the miners' steps in those days. I'd go down the steps and off to the reed beds and, you know, check the siphons and alternate the flow between different reed beds so that they don't get too much sewage on them, so they get this pulsated flow, so they grow nicely. You'd be down there, and it's just so beautiful, a really nice place to be, and then walk back up the steps and peak knock the compost toilet. When people poo in the compost toilet it kind of makes a poo mountain and you have to knock the poo mountain flat with this specially derived kind of plank on the end of a shovel called a peak knocker."

Louise Halestrap

Ecological water and sewage treatment is still one of CAT's most successful outputs (as it were) and has inspired many individuals and organisations over the years – from the National Trust to Prince Charles. Water collected in the reservoir is treated using slow sand filtration methods, used minimally on site with priority given to essential use, and treated again after use, using low energy ecological cleaning systems (reed beds), before being allowed to flow back into the river. Visitors can see the systems in action and recreate effectively at home. Whereas domestic scale wind turbines in most urban areas are inadvisable, a compost toilet at the end of the garden or allotment (if the allotment rules allow it) is perfectly feasible.

"We got quite a range of reactions to compost toilets. Working in the biology department I was quite often doing guided tours. You were trying to show five or six people or more a compost toilet, so you're actually trying to cram a lot of people into a very small toilet, which everybody finds quite amusing. And people outside find it quite bizarre when lots and lots of people are sort of walking out of a toilet. Most people were quite open to the idea that they might work in certain situations. Sewage is never a one size fits all approach so showing people a good variety of options was a good thing. It's a very personal thing, what your sanitary standard is. It's got to be a facility you're willing to use. We had one particular sewage system at the eco-cabins where the main part of the sewage system was actually in a poly-tunnel. And there was always tomato plants growing in there and, because the tomato itself wouldn't have ever have been in contact with the sewage, we could harvest the tomatoes and make it into sewage tomato chutney. There was never very much of it but it was quite a special thing to have sewage tomato chutney. It would say sewage tomato chutney on the label and it would be sat on the shelf in tea chest, which at that point was still the site community kitchen, and you could have the annual batch of sewage tomato chutney."

Judith Thornton, aka Dr Bog

URINE

is full of valuable plant foods. It is particularly useful as an activator in compost heaps. So, gentlemen, please contribute generously.

PEE HERE

Appendix B for photo captions

Chapter 2

Sense of place

"What has had a real change on the feel of the place, is that when I was first at CAT, way pre-computer, pre-mobile phones, pre-satellite TV, pre-all those sort of things, is that it felt incredibly remote, particularly in the winter. I mean, it really did feel remote, because, well, you couldn't get a TV picture. There were all these attempts. People would take aerials right up into the hills and have all these cables coming down, which would work fine until some moisture got into it, which wouldn't take long. And even when you did get a picture it would be this incredibly snowy thing that wasn't worth watching. We got *The Guardian* each day. That was contact with the outside world. Even buying things was pretty difficult. Once a week the market was really important, so if you wanted to get clothes that was the place to go. The thing is [because of that] we all looked the same. We all wore the same clothes. There was a lot of these alpaca jumpers … a lot of us had brown wellies for a while."

Rick Dance

© Cristian Barnett / Collins

As the box on page 32 illustrates, Gerard started CAT with the backing of industrialists and politicians, along with £20,000 funding from his half brother Robert Morgan-Grenville. He sent an American named Steve Boulter around the UK to find a site. After several rejections Steve arrived at the disused Llwyngwern Quarry in the winter of 1973 – via a chance encounter with a group called Earth Workshop. The quarry was located in a remote Welsh community inhabiting the slopes of the Dulas Valley, named after the river that tumbles through it.

No doubt Steve Boulter spent several hours walking around the quarry on his first visit but it probably didn't take that long for him to realise that Llwyngwern Quarry (roughly translated, Llwyn Gwern means Alder Grove) was exactly what he was looking for. As he later recalled in *Undercurrents* magazine, "It had just the combination of wind, water, sun, space and surroundings that we were after. It came equipped with all the essentials, including 6000 square feet of ancestral slate cutting sheds, three cottages, two streams and reservoirs, assorted tunnels, a bit of railway, and several thousand tonnes of slate of assorted sizes and shapes."[1]

The several thousand tonnes of slate described here were actually pieces of slate waste dug out of the original quarry over one hundred years of hard labour, carried out through a small tunnel from the original quarry onto the railway track and tipped onto what must have once been grassy fields kept for sheep. Most of the good stuff had long since been shipped out and used to make billiard tables, fireplaces, floors and other heavy objects such as pig troughs. What was left had been piled up to form a fairly flat but uneven expanse of post-industrial wasteland onto which had fallen the seeds of trees, shrubs, brambles and wild flowers, all of which had grown profusely over the fifteen years since the quarry had been abandoned by commerce.

The average visitor to such a site would have wondered what they had stumbled upon, and having admired its craggy bleakness and the tenacity of its plant life for a short while, beaten a hasty retreat back down the single lane farm track to whatever comfortable slice of life they had found for themselves elsewhere. Those who had allowed adventure to fall into their souls may have spent a few hours clambering over its rocks, discovering its multiple ruins and proudly standing on its viewpoints admiring Tarren-y-Gesail, the glorious but quite often cloud-shrouded mountain that stands in spectacular coincidence opposite.

---

1 *Undercurrents* 07/04 1974,
   http://issuu.com/undercurrents1972/docs/uc_on_cat_may26a

They may even have taken a plunge into the deep cold reservoir of water once kept in readiness to power the machinery used to cut the slate, but now abandoned and left to the pond skaters and horseflies. They may have brushed away cobwebs to poke a head through a cottage door, to place a foot on a sponge-rotten floorboard, to look up and witness the sky through missing slate tiles. They may have noticed the damp patches and the crumbling stains of weathered paint, plaster torn from lath, the woodlice and the wrens, mice and rats, slug trails and the taste of disintegration.

Beyond the cottages they may have come to the narrow arched entrance of a tunnel, long enough not to see the light at the end of it and dark enough to need a torch, which, if they had one, they could have held up to its jagged, rough-cut slate edges and then pointed downwards to the puddle strewn tip toe floor, so as not to trip or graze their head or shoulder.

You can still emerge from the other side as Steve Boulter did that day in 1973 to see the same sight, although now all the more verdant and overgrown with fern, rhododendron, willow, alder, hazel and other herbaceous guests that have found themselves protected from the rest of the world in this deep, cavernous, still, damp and – apart from the small mammals, insects, birds and reptiles that call it home – foot free space. Not even the sheep visit.

"There's something very magical about the quarry. The best time to go is in the wintertime when there's been lots of frost. I remember going down there one day, on my own, when it was a sunny morning in the winter and there were icicles just hanging down all around. You can stand in the middle, because it's like a big drum, and you stand in the middle and you can hear the icicles creaking, and it's the most incredible thing to do on a winter morning. I don't know if it's still possible, it might be too overgrown around the edges but then there was still bare slate on the quarry sides, which would hold the icicles. There's nothing like these icicles creaking and then of course, they start to drop and they crash down, so it's a completely um, er, fantastic experience. You just feel like you've just been transported out of this world."

Jane Bryant

Although CAT started off as the National Centre for Alternative Technology it soon became known simply as the Quarry. The Quarry refers to the whole site, including the waste tip on which all the social and economic activity happens, but the 'old quarry' (note lower case q) is the actual source of all the slate and thus the wellspring from which CAT sprung. To many people who worked at CAT the old quarry is regarded almost as a sacred space, as well as being potentially the most dangerous place on site. Nothing very much 'human' happens there. We journey into it with light footsteps occasionally but mostly it is left to nature, and has been now for almost 60 years. It is a very special place.

Artist in residence Glenn Davidson and I spent four hours listening to and recording the quarry one evening, the recordings eventually forming the backdrop to a 'sonic poem' Glenn created with the voice of one of our interviewees, CAT's first technical director and innovative engineer Bob Todd. It's better heard than read (www.artstation.org.uk/CAT/CAT.html) but the sonic signatures in the quarry recordings make the connection between Bob's early formative experiences, his work at the Quarry and the soundscape of the quarry, distilling an essence of Bob's voice and story from two hours of interview.

Ariana Jordão and another project volunteer, Jane Lloyd Francis, later created an immersive performance in the quarry called Cerdded Llwyngwern (Lwyngwern Walk). During the performance participants were invited to take a guided walk through the tunnel and into the quarry where they encountered storytellers and meaningful objects during a one-hour reflection on history, industry and the natural world. Launched on CAT's 40th anniversary open day and performed again during the 2014 members' conference, the piece allowed participants to enter a space normally barred to visitors and to re-discover CAT's cavernous past.

The physicality of CAT is an important part of its history, both in terms of its location in the rugged, wet and climatically dramatic landscapes of mid-Wales and also in the sustained efforts needed to turn a disused quarry into a home.

The adventurous visitor may stay for a few hours and take advantage of the quarry's various wild spots, but it takes another leap of faith and imagination to believe that you could stay, live and at the same time create a stunning new vision of the future there.

```
Bob Todd sonic poem one
              by Glenn Davidson

     Sonic signatures: water drops falling
     in tunnel, bird song, walking on slate.


                   "Fortunately my dad was interested
                   in electrical stuff...

             ...but I remember from a very
             early age making crystal
             set radios, winding
             coils on jam jars and
             all that sort of stuff...

                   ...helped to make some of my early
                   efforts positive and work...

           ...otherwise it could have been quite
           discouraging and I might have given up."
```

"[The first site manager Tony Williams] was looking at this
completely derelict site. Even the engine shed had no roof.
He had extraordinary fortitude to even think about tackling it
because there was virtually no money; there was no person,
there was nothing there."

Rod James

"I'm from Glamorgan. I moved here more or less the same time
as CAT. I'd been on this site before anybody at CAT had been
here. I left my footprints here. We sort of grew up together
in this part of the country. Very, very hostile environment.
I remember coming down years ago with my next-door
neighbour Richie. He was 74. He saw some boys trying to shift

some stones, and he'd worked in slate most of his life, and he thought he'd give them a hand and they couldn't believe the things he was lifting. But he knew how to lift slate. These were Oxford and Cambridge graduates and they had no idea how to work physically."

Donald Bennett

"It just rained incessantly, day in, day out and, I remember, I was living in a caravan at the bottom of the track. [It] leaked, um, and I just remember, climbing every night, into a sopping wet bed, and getting up in the morning and putting on these sopping wet clothes … day after day after day, and that at that time, we even somehow, we hadn't quite, I don't quite understand our intelligence or what was going on, but we hadn't even thought of lighting a fire to dry the clothes or dry the bedding or anything. We just had our minds absolutely set on, on the work in hand, you know, just clearing the track away."

Jill Whitehead

And yet, the fact that CAT emerged from a disused quarry could well have been the making of it, because it allowed for the creation of a phoenix mythology. If you could create this vision for the future on the most earth-torn of landscapes, and show that you could enhance nature whilst delivering sustained economic and social activity on a site most people had given up on, you could show that it was possible to turn around any desperate situation with imagination, hope and fortitude.

"It was the early seventies and CAT was just like a heaven. We walked into this lovely place, beautiful place, where we could build our own world. I didn't need to go anywhere else when I got here. I couldn't believe how beautiful it was. Idyllic. The mountains and the rivers and the trees. We seemed to fit in just right and we had one of the cottages. We were on site for twelve years. There was a good smallholding. We had loads of chickens. We had ducks and goats and we did get cows. We ended up with two milking cows. Pigs. We went into pigs. Buying weaners, fattening them up and then killing them and eating the meat. Of course it was always a very emotional time when the pigs had to go. Alternative technology implies machines, doesn't it, somehow, but the green I think was nearly as important as the windmills and the solar panels, growing your food. We used the manure from the animals, and we killed the animals and ate some of the meat. Since then I've become a vegetarian but at the time we shared the meat around. I do remember me and Jeremy [Light] killing a calf, which I think was quite tricky. I remember going off finding two geese, and they bred, and we had thirteen young geese all walking in a line behind mum and dad; was the most amazing sight. We ended up with 90 chickens at its peak I think. I think it's always been high on people's lists of what did they enjoy. I think some of the gardens have impressed people, as well as disappointed some, because my gardens tend to be rather wild (laughs). Not quite National Trust. For many years I did a salad for the workers at CAT every day. Me and the volunteers; for years. We had these huge bowls of mixed salads. I was trying to show people what they could grow. How beautiful it was and how wonderful food it is, and feed everybody at CAT, and so in theory make everyone healthy, so we could do our job better. Really, that was my vision."

Roger McLennan

'Built on a disused quarry in mid-Wales' became a phrase central to any press release, talk or TV programme about CAT. It automatically intrigued people. Who would want to live in an old slate quarry? They must be doing something meaningful, eccentric or ridiculous. Either way it helped to engage people with the mission.

"We watched the news one night, together, and we saw a small item about people looking at sustainable living at a slate quarry in Wales. We saw it on BBC2 news and it didn't look very attractive. It was pouring with rain as usual in Wales, and they mentioned that they wanted volunteers. So a year, about a year later, when we were on holiday in the area, we thought we'd go and look and see what was happening, and sure enough it was raining again and there were a load of people digging in the slate, and we volunteered."

Liz Todd

"People like [movie star] Julie Christie came. She brought her father I remember. God it was exciting here – the fact that she would take an interest in it. But she didn't come as 'I'm Julie Christie on a red carpet', she just arrived because she just thought that was rather fun."

Rod James

Idealistically, the location also sat well with Gerard's stated intention of supporting the Alternative Technology (AT) philosophy of decentralisation (see box on page 59) but perhaps more importantly: pragmatically, with a rent of 5p per annum and a supportive landlord (who coincidently knew Gerard from Eton), it was perfect for an organisation that had no discernible plan of how it would finance its own existence beyond the first year, or even exactly what it would do in the longer term. Plus Gerard had already tried to secure several sites in other more accessible locations and failed.

There is no mention in the founding documents of how CAT might relate to the indigenous culture that would surround it: one person's decentralisation quite possibly being another's English imperialism. There is no reference to Welsh cultural values, the Welsh language or local engagement. In fact, apart from mentioning the local railway station, there is only one mention of the locality: '8h) There is labour available locally'.

In fact there was already a strong anti-nuclear movement in Wales, as well as long-standing peace movements and anti-establishment movements for the promotion of the Welsh language, culture and devolution. It's probably fair to say that the site and the mission interested Gerard more than the cultural and political landscape of Wales.

It's possible that this lack of knowledge about the Welsh political and cultural landscape hindered CAT's integration in the local area and perhaps even hindered the cause of environmentalism on a local level. But there was also plenty of support for CAT locally, not only from many local people but also from prominent figures within Wales such as Assembly Member Dafydd Ellis Thomas (not yet interviewed) and former Plaid Cymru MP, CAT Trustee and oral history interviewee Cynog Dafis.

From the start, reactions to CAT were mixed. On the one hand local resident and CAT neighbour Betty Jones 'the Mill', who much later, in the words of Peter Harper, "became a champion of acceptance and integration", was reported to have taken a petition up and down the Dulas valley to prevent CAT from starting up. On the other, many other local people were interested in what CAT was doing, visited their new neighbours and generously offered support in various ways.

Audrey Beaumont (interviewed) was CAT's landlord but was more like a mother. There are constant reminders of her and her late husband John's generosity towards CAT in a diary kept throughout 1974. They donated furniture and clean clothes, accommodated visitors and even cooked cakes for Prince Philip, who visited CAT in 1974.

But some people refused to visit or accept work there.

> "There were people that wouldn't go there to work. There was a lot of people still, I don't know what the word is, just didn't like the idea of hippies being on their patch or something, I don't know."
>
> *Edward Jones*

And if you were a local person who did accept work at CAT you could yourself be questioned about what you were doing up there. Delyth Rees went to CAT to teach Welsh originally and was invited to become a trustee, a post she was very proud to accept, and kept for over fifteen years. She is familiar with the history of mid-Wales and speaks in her interview of the accommodation of waves of immigrants for hundreds of years, from the Huguenots of the 17th and 18th centuries through to the quarry workers of the late 19th and early 20th centuries.

"Many [local people] were suspicious thinking, and asking me, 'What are you doing in Pantperthog with all those hippies there?' That's how they saw them at the time; there was us and them. But now many people from the Centre have become a part of our community, have taught the language to their children, have gone to Welsh schools and are enriching our culture. They compete in the National Eisteddfod, as you know. And lately in Powys Eisteddfod there was a party singing 'Bonheddwr Mawr y Bala' on the stage brilliantly. And well, you, Sally, have been president of our branch of Merched y Wawr. And have learnt Welsh."[2]

Delyth Rees

Those people that did cross the Rubicon often became vocal supporters of CAT and quite often turned out to be crucial to CAT's development, farmer and engineer Edward Jones and master craftsman and poet Eirig Humphries being two examples. Eirig worked at CAT throughout the 1970s and was responsible for re-building many of the derelict slate structures. You can still see his work, as solid and beautiful now as it was when it was built over 35 years ago. Eirig died many years ago and I never had the opportunity to meet or interview him but the high regard with which people held him is clear in interviews.

"He was the most lovely man. He was very quiet. He had a beautiful lilt to his voice and he was walking poetry. It was like watching poetry to watch Eirig. He always moved very slowly and he would stand quietly considering his next project, the wall he was having to build ... He would never pick a piece [of slate] up and decide it was rubbish and put it back. Everything was economical and necessary. You always felt he could see so much more than you in the landscape. He was a lovely, gentle fellow."

Jane Bryant

---

[2]   Eisteddfod is the most important cultural event held in the Welsh language. Bonheddwr Mawr y Bala translates as Great Gentlemen of Bala. Merched y Wawr, 'Daughters of the Dawn', is a voluntary non-political organisation for women in Wales, similar to the Women's Institute. The Sally in this quote is interviewer and CAT fundraiser Sally Carr, also mentioned in Thea Platt's quote on page 100.

Edward Jones was interviewed. He helped CAT complete many of its most complicated engineering projects and later went on to build what was at the time Europe's largest wind farm, a few miles from CAT.

"If I'm honest, probably I should have been a full-time engineer. My heart always lied with the technical side of tractors and machinery but because I was born to a farming family there's a certain amount of pressure to keep the farm going. I don't regret any of that but my interest was in engineering mainly, so I always made sure that all work was done with the minimum sweat really, if it meant using a machine or adapting something, so that was my, that's the way I thought at the time, and to be involved with CAT gave me a lot of opportunity really, to develop skills and ideas. I had a lot of experience with machinery and working on slopes, and so getting a windmill up a hill and laying the cables down the slopes was, I thoroughly enjoyed really."

Edward Jones

'CAT's relationship with local people', 'CAT's effect on the Dyfi Valley' and 'CAT's impact on the use of the Welsh language' all became important areas of interest as the oral history project developed, as did the impact the Dyfi Valley had on incomers coming to work at CAT, and their children.

There is no clear-cut statement that sums up the cross-cultural experiences of all the people interviewed for the project, as they are very diverse. Integration became easier as children went to school and learned Welsh, encouraging their parents to take Welsh lessons too. Some 'Quarry kids' were bullied at school in the early days but there was also plenty of mixing and the emergence of great friendships. The New Dyfi Players' pantomime brought many people together as CAT's technical and theatrical skills and enthusiasm proved valuable assets. A tradition of self-written pantomime scripts emerged after CAT's third director, Pete Raine, created *Rats* in the 1980s, a pantomime based on the story of the Pied Piper.

"I think it became one of the major ways in which the Quarry integrated into the town. My last year here I wound up in Bronglais hospital for about three weeks and they wouldn't let me go home (laughs), and I thought, 'I'm really bored so I'm going to write a musical'. So I wrote a musical called *Rats*, which was a rock musical based on the Pied Piper of Hamelin. Phil Wheeler [local fabric shop owner and musician] did the music and I did the lyrics and directed it. And we self wrote a pantomime. And that tradition carried on. I left in '86 and it was still going in the mid '90s."

Pete Raine

Many of the interviewees thought CAT had brought a great deal of money into the area, created jobs, supported local businesses and given the town a more cosmopolitan feel. A study of the economic impact of CAT and off shoots like Dulas Engineering and Ecodyfi is long overdue. Pete Raine – at one point in the mid 1980s – worked out that the Quarry was responsible for 5% of the total GDP of the Dyfi Valley. CAT's presence in the area is economically unconventional, in that most of the early funding for it was sourced through donations rather than government subsidy or private investment. Such a study, then, would have to include comparisons to traditional government investment schemes in the area, some of which have failed.

It's clear that CAT has had, in some ways, a negative impact on the use of spoken Welsh in the Valley because CAT brought in an influx of non-Welsh speakers. This made it harder for Welsh to be the language of choice at some public events and meetings and even in small group conversations.

"As time goes on and numbers grow, concern about dilution of Welsh language life starts to grow. If there were clubs and societies, which previously might have been run in Welsh, and then English speakers turn up, what happens? Does the whole thing turn to English because the one person can't cope with the Welsh? Yes, often. It gradually reduces the arena in which Welsh is the natural medium of communication. It's not just the influence of incomers, but the influence of the media.

The English culture is so strong, being the stronger next-door neighbour as expressed through television, radio, the internet and everything else. It is the dominant medium, so throughout Wales that has had to be addressed. And it is also very complex in terms of the attitudes of Welsh speakers to the Welsh language versus the English language. That's gone through change from a situation where not that long ago it was frowned on to pass on Welsh to your kids because English was the language of progress, and anything else would hold them back. That's left a legacy now of Welsh people feeling almost disenfranchised within Wales because they haven't got the Welsh language. What is Wales and Welsh identity? I found myself [Whilst working there in the 1980s and 90s] being critical of other CAT staff who didn't seem to notice that they were in Wales and indeed they might well have been in rural Cornwall or the Lake District for all the effort they made to notice that or do anything about it. Being originally English myself I know that Welsh doesn't register really on the political or social awareness scale [in England] – it's just another part of England really for most people – and doesn't register in the London-based media and you don't learn about it at school, and then you come here and you think, um gosh what is this, people are speaking this language. But if you don't actually spend much time off site you don't come across the Welsh language or Welsh people much, so you haven't got that stimulus, so it's fairly easy to remain insular. And there was no attempt to tell people otherwise in terms of induction process coming on to the CAT staff, it just didn't really register as being part of the mission in those days. So it was a big ignorance rather than anything wilful, and it's taken quite a long time to grow that consciousness and awareness, that that dimension is interesting and important and that CAT not only has a mission to speak to the world but a mission to be relevant to the local community."

Andy Rowland

In the past there have been examples of cultural insensitivity towards the Welsh language that have deeply upset some people. Some of the interviewees also recalled that some people at CAT had told them that they considered it more important to spend their time fighting environmental campaigns rather than learning Welsh. On the other hand, as Delyth Rees notes on page 55, many people at CAT have learnt or continue to learn Welsh.

"I don't know whether Welsh is a very difficult language to learn, but a lot of the people that were there [in the 1980s and 90s], I would ask them sometimes, what did the Welsh language mean to them, but a lot of the time the answer would be that their time would be better spent encouraging renewable thoughts and ideas than learning the language, really, so probably a bit disappointed in that sense. I did sympathise with them. But, to keep a language you've got to use it."

Edward Jones

Supporting a philosophy of decentralisation

The Society for Environmental Improvement was the parent charity set up to establish CAT. Its founding document (available on-line at archive.cat.org.uk) sets out its operating principles and goals. In this short extract the document's authors (unidentified) set out the need for decentralisation:

"There is also a growing awareness that the administrative and manufacturing centralisation necessary to sustain rapid material expansion is dehumanising people. Individual choices are becoming even narrower as dependence on, and conformity [to] central systems increases ... The consequence is a growing need for a more self-sufficient life-style.

A.T. [alternative technology] is a direct step towards this aim. Its employment is being seen not only as a technical solution to current problems, but as a philosophical alternative to man's obsession with material expansion and its inevitable association with economic breakdown and social chaos ... For this reason a site well away from a major town is preferable."

chop it
cook it
eat it

a Beginner's guide to wholefood cookery, from the quarry shop.

See Appendix B for photo captions

The Quarry Café and Shop in Machynlleth

"I suppose because food has always been my original path in to here, and wholefoods and vegetarianism, I always felt that they were part of the whole package. For those seven years I worked at the Café I was very happy. In a way I've never seen it as going to work, it's always just been part of what I do."

Annie Lowmass

The Quarry Café and Shop were both set up in 1979 to form a bridge between the Quarry and the town, and to promote vegetarianism and whole food. At first some local people were suspicious of the Quarry Café and Shop, just as they were suspicious of the Quarry.

"A lot of local people didn't come in. I'd sit and talk to people in the pub and they'd say, 'I'd like to come in but I daren't, it's too different.' People have said to me, 'I got to the door but I just chickened out.' Some girls would come in to eat. The boys would come and stand at the door eating their chips and sort of talk but they wouldn't come through [the door]."

Nigel Dudley

One legend has it that this started to change when a local doctor started recommending prunes for the encouragement of bowel movements, but I really don't know if this is true or not! In any case a steady stream of people started to venture inside, local people took jobs there, and the Quarry Shop and Café became popular institutions in the town, offering something a bit different, a difference that was appreciated. It is hard to underestimate how important the Quarry Café and Shop were in building a connection between the town and CAT, and how much love there is in the town for them.

"I think originally it enabled CAT to merge into the local life. Local people could get jobs here and local people could visit. Everybody's welcome. You get quite a wide variety of customers. Lots and lots of local people come in from all walks of life. Professional people – teachers and the bank people, the dentist. Then we've got the market stall holders every week. It just seems to appeal to a wide range of people, who use it regularly. I think they feel quite fond of it. Feels like a second home really. I think it's quite comfortable. A lot of staff are Welsh speakers so we get a lot of Welsh-speaking local people in as well. It does have lots and lots of regulars."

Lynda Wenman

The Café and Shop were closed in January 2013 due to financial problems with CAT's PLC. The closure created a huge sense of shock and sadness in Machynlleth. During the day of the closure people gathered outside the Café to stare at the hastily erected hand-written sign informing them that it was closing down. I went myself and once again was reminded of how much the town loved the Café and Shop, as people, such as the then mayor Gareth Jones (not yet interviewed) stopped to ask me what was going on and to say how terrible it was.

But there is a happy ending to this story. The staff of both the Shop and the Café took control of their businesses and, within a few months and to unalloyed joy, re-opened them, the Quarry Café where it was previously and the shop relocated a few doors down the high street with the new name Dyfi Wholefoods.

"That went on for some time, people being sad and missing it. A real void. It was really horrible. That was January. St David's Day [March 1st] is the café's anniversary, so I put a St David's Day card on the door just to say Happy St David's Day and to say we wish we were open. We finally got the keys by the end of April. We had a week before the comedy festival started, and on Friday we opened. People were helping just painting and a few people from CAT were really helpful. We couldn't have done it without them. [Opening again] was really amazing and nerve wracking and exciting. We were really, really, really happy. It was really sunny and people started to mingle outside the door. We said, 'Come on, we'll line up and open the door all together', so we were all holding arms, went to the door and opened it and people came in. Some of the staff were crying, and people hugging, flowers and cards, lovely, the mayor. It was really, really nice. Felt really good and it's just been really busy ever since."

Lynda Wenman

Think Global, Act Local

Anne Marie Carty and Dan Gifford – two of our artists in residence – explored many of these 'sense of place' themes in a three-month project that included a two-week bicycle tour of community spaces and village halls up and down the Dulas and Dyfi valleys. At each event they invited members of the local community to watch a video they had created mixing archive footage of local Eisteddfod festivals, markets and country fairs, borrowed from the National Library, and clips taken from the oral history interviews and old TV programmes about CAT.

After each screening the audience was invited to respond to it on camera. These filmed responses then formed the basis of a second film that was then shown to CAT staff, who were also filmed responding to it. This created an iterative responsive process that allowed us to build up a picture of what people felt about local issues.

The informal atmosphere of the screenings provided local people and CAT staff the space to reflect on their own lives, the local community and CAT's place in it. It allowed an indirect conversation to take place between local people and CAT staff, suggesting how CAT can still be relevant to the local community, even after 40 years. It also allowed people to express any criticisms they might have of CAT, whilst celebrating its achievements and showing the love and pride they had for it. Even amongst people who were initially sceptical about CAT there was a lot of pride that CAT was based in their area. The chance to have these sorts of conversations was incredibly important, as they provided a forum for people to talk about things that meant a great deal to them.

This process also allowed us to extend the reach of the oral history project from 80 to well over 300 people, drawing in many people we wouldn't otherwise have been able to interview. The interviews are not in-depth, and are collective and responsive to the situation and the people around them, but they do offer a unique contribution to our knowledge about the Dyfi Valley in 2014. The many hours of recorded footage are now archived at the National Library.

See Appendix B for photo captions

Chapter 3

Community, conflict and co-operation

"I'd thought my job was to work out a plan for the gardens, but I could quite quickly see that was not a very tactful thing to do and so I realised it was better to join the rest and hump concrete up a hill."

Jeremy Light

"The ogre had absolute authority. We had a rotating ogre so that different people did it. But of course different people had different standards. The problem is that on the whole, people living at the Quarry got used to a standard which was completely different to society. It was so grubby and scrappy. It was workable but it didn't really make sense. The ogre's job was to try and keep the public displays looking good but Gerard would come in with an outside view wanting to hit standards which clearly other people there really didn't recognise. A lot of us were only one step away from students.

All of us were 23, 24. One hadn't ever had to build a house or decorate it or actually do things neatly in a way that society was doing it. [Gerard] was 37. He lived in a Georgian house. It was smart, and he was selling upmarket silverware. But he was far more representative of society."

Rod James

CAT maintained a long-term commitment to co-operative working principles for thirty-seven years. These working structures were established and refined under the leadership of the second director, Rod James, between 1975 and 1980 and changed over time as the organisation grew. In that early period they included the following operating principles and systems:

- Consensus decision making at open weekly meetings.

- 'Being the boss for a week': this role, known as 'the Ogre' (see quote above), went with considerable powers and was also rotated.

- The sharing of communal jobs through a rota system, including visitor reception, cooking, bread making and toilet cleaning.

- Opportunities to step out of defined roles to help the collective.

- Shared management responsibility.

- A flat basic wage with extra discretionary payments for those with children and those particularly in need.

- Communal lunch for everyone and, for those who lived on site, shared evening meals (both almost always vegetarian).

- An organised volunteer programme that enabled others to experience and contribute to co-operative working practices and communal living.

The values that lay behind the co-operative structure at CAT can fairly be called radical because they offered a genuine affront to conventional organisational models; they were, and are still, barely known or understood outside the co-operative movement. Unions, corporations, governments, armies, religious organisations – in fact almost all social structures – operate using hierarchical systems. The idea that the director was included on a rota for cleaning the toilets was genuinely shocking to many people.

"In my ten years at CAT there was only one occasion where a decision couldn't be made by consensus. So I am actually still a staunch defender of consensus. I still believe in it absolutely. I think it's a very important principle. Of all the reasons I loved the job – and it was by far the best ten-year period of my working life – was the whole co-operative work ethos. You were sharing both the benefits and the liabilities with a whole group of other people so it was never a question of 'the buck stops with me'. But I do accept that it is not the right thing for everybody. My brother-in-law had been in personnel management (HR) all his life and he said, 'If we tried doing that in our business you would find that probably less than 10% of the workforce had any interest in taking on any responsibility.' That's what he told me, and I suspect that's true for a large part of the workforce as a whole. While I'm still a great believer in co-ops I'm more realistic about how much the co-operative work ethos can penetrate into the economy as a whole. It was always a source of satisfaction to me that I actually spent quite a lot of time cleaning the public toilets at CAT. I actually liked doing it because I really believed that everybody should have their share of doing it. I didn't want to be in a position where I was exempt from doing that and other people did simply because they had a different job title."

Roger Kelly

The co-operative way of working at CAT gave some people a sense of deep connection to ideas, life experiences and other people. Several interviewers described their lives as being in two halves: pre-CAT and post-CAT. One interviewee described his time at CAT as like discovering colour TV after living in black and white.

> "It's kind of almost as if life began at CAT, like life before CAT and life after CAT being completely different. It's almost like, you know, coming into colour television."
>
> *Mark Bloomfield*

> "There was life pre-CAT and life post-CAT, and probably most people think like that."
>
> *Sally Oakes*

> "For me personally it had a massively positive effect. I feel like the way I now think and the ten years of my life since being at CAT [have] all been coloured by my experience at CAT so I do feel like I owe CAT a big debt."
>
> *Jake Voelcker*

CAT's open approach was particularly beneficial for many of the women interviewed, who quite often experienced a profound sense of empowerment during their time there, either because the spirit of CAT encouraged them to participate more fully in jobs that would normally be the preserve of men (hard physical labour and practical outdoor jobs such as building and engineering) or because the flat management structure enabled women to play central roles in a way that traditional male-dominated hierarchies did not. I remember being the only man on the Overview management board with four women – Deirdre Raffan, Sue Cameron, Cindy Harris (interviewed) and Annie Lowmass (interviewed).

"I saw an advert for a woman builder, and I remember thinking: my god somebody wants a woman builder. If it had just been an ad for a builder I probably wouldn't have registered it. Ewan [Barker] said he was leaving and there was this discussion about replacing him, and Jean Welstead and I think probably Claire [second name unknown] made the argument for couching the adverts in terms of positive discrimination. I'm sure there were arguments against, as there always are. 'Ooh we don't want any type of discrimination.' [Being at CAT] was immensely rewarding. As I say, I wasn't that confident when I came to CAT, but I got huge confidence, and I think took forward the whole thinking on environmental building materials in particular, as part of the CAT message. Using the resources, the freedom, the autonomy that we were given but very much trying to deliver back to CAT a message it could carry forward. The good times were really amazing."

Cindy Harris

"I'd just turned 24. As a young woman turning up to CAT, I don't think I was conscious of it, but that was essential for my coming to being, that liberation. I could just do what I chose because my gender isn't an obstacle. If I want to pick up a hammer or if I want to chop some wood it's not only possible, it's expected."

Hele Oakley

"[Before coming to work at CAT] I had one of those epiphany moments, on a Saturday night coming back from the West End, sitting on the number twenty seven bus, when I suddenly felt some pride in my achievements, previously having been slightly, ehm, reticent and a bit ashamed of just being a secretary. I then realised, well in that case I could probably do something else as well, and went to the office on Monday and handed in my notice. [I remember] my boss saying 'So what are you going to do?' and I said, 'Actually I've got no idea, and moreover I don't care, I just want out.'"

Irene Gallant

This does not mean that CAT created some sort of gender-equal utopia. While some experienced the dismantling of traditional gender roles, others found themselves inhabiting them, especially in the early days.

"I didn't want to come and live in a community, and I didn't want to come here at all but I came because I wanted to be with Jeremy. I felt, always an outsider, because being a mother, I was the only one with a young child. There were a lot of young people, young women who were very physically able and active and seemed to be really enjoying themselves, doing concreting and lots of physical tasks, up the mountains, and I felt, I felt when they came down they looked at me and thought, 'Oh she's not done anything all day', and I felt, having a baby is quite hard work, in these conditions."

Gayle Light

"The men we were involved with had made a specific decision to take a job at CAT, often downsizing and dropping salary. We women found ourselves not only married to the man but to the Quarry as well. The pay was low and many of us had to take on work as well, and we didn't get as much help with childcare as we might have originally hoped for. You know, if you are touring around giving keynote speeches, writing articles, books, being filmed, invited abroad...well how exciting compared to holding the fort/nappy bucket/compost bin back home. The minutia of daily life became boring and distracted from 'Saving the Planet'. For all that, it has been a pleasure to see so many creative, adventurous, inspired, caring, talented children blossom out of the Quarry World."

Janet Davies

Holdfast, the women's oral history project created by Ariana Jordão and Rosie Leach – and funded by the Women's Equality Network Wales – explored some of these themes in oral history based performance and extended group interviews for International Women's Day and the National Library archive launch event. Using clips from the oral history interviews they were able to show how diverse the experiences of women at CAT were.

The freedom to participate was enshrined in CAT's folklore. You came, you got involved, and when you left you took some of the spirit of CAT with you: into the jobs that followed, the relationships you formed, the communities you became part of. This is reflected in the kinds of organisations that people started at CAT or went on to form or join after leaving.

Dulas Engineering is a case in point. Born out of the spirit of co-operation and social change found at CAT in the 1970s and 80s, Dulas Engineering was set up to manufacture control systems for renewable energy and solar refrigeration units for hard-to-reach regions in the developing world – at the time a marginal concern to most people.

"Within a year of starting we were making data-logging equipment to send to Kenya and we were using it to monitor the performance of pumping water with wind power, and that was the thing that really enthused me: that there were things that I was working on that would make a very big difference to people's lives. I'm interested in what sort of difference [the technology] can make, either to climate change or people's welfare."

Jo Gwillim

When CAT felt like it could no longer sustain a manufacturing unit inside the organisation, Dulas took off as an independent co-operative and is now one of the most important medium-sized renewable energy companies in Britain.

Other 'spin-offs' include globally important company Aber Instruments, still run with a socially engaged attitude towards pay differentials, and the Centre for Sustainable Energy in Bristol (originally UCAT – the Urban Centre for Alternative Technology), which is still committed to social improvement and community-scale energy initiatives.

This tradition of innovation stems from the early days of CAT and has continued throughout its history – the spirit of communally-controlled, enterprise-generating initiatives, projects and businesses that take on a life of their own. We could call many of CAT's own enterprises 'spin-ons' – departments that were started through the individual or collective initiatives of the staff: Buy Green By Mail (now CAT Ecostore), CAT Publications, the Graduate School of the Environment, the Eco-cabins.

Then there are the countless businesses, organisations and opportunities that have been created by the many volunteers, students and members who have defined their commitment to the world partly as a result of time spent at CAT: Cwm Einion Organic Growers (one of Britain's first organic veg box schemes); This is Rubbish (campaigning anti food waste group); Building Is Everything (creators of pop-up architecture events).

But it's easy to paint an overly rosy image of the co-operative system at CAT. It could also be very frustrating, slow and even unjust – particularly as the number of people employed by CAT grew. It did not eliminate political infighting, power groupings, resentment or feelings of marginalisation. The consensus decision-making process that evolved at CAT was quite often little understood by new members of staff, who found it hard to get their head 'round how it all worked, and sometimes used by members of staff – we all had the power to 'block' decisions – to override the wishes of the majority.

As CAT grew, the open Monday meetings disappeared and were replaced by an elected management group called Overview and a monthly permanent staff meeting (PSM). To maintain the consensus principle a process emerged that allowed people to object to decisions made by Overview and force the issue with which they were concerned to be heard by everyone at the monthly PSMs.

Because everyone had to agree, it did at times feel undemocratic, in the sense that the will of the majority could be overridden by the power of a single individual. Having said this, most of the time most of the people respected the democratic majority and withdrew their block if the feeling in the room was against them, merely requesting a note to be taken in the minutes that they didn't agree with the decision. This allowed their views to be registered.

The system did, however, favour people who were more extrovert and not afraid to stand up and make their voices heard at large meetings. Most people who had no experience of this kind of meeting at the beginning gained confidence over the years, but some people found themselves unable to fully participate. The meetings themselves could be dramatic, emotional, exhaustingly long and – unless you had kept up with a sequence of minutes preceding the meeting – often confusing.

> "I think there was a place for introverts there but I think it was more of a challenge for people who were shier to cope with that sort of work practice. I do think it was challenging for someone who was quite shy and maybe that wasn't really recognised that much. But I don't know if there's anything you can do to help someone who doesn't like public speaking. I did struggle with the thought of 'Oh my god I have to speak in front of all these people.' I didn't really enjoy going to the meetings."
>
> *Lynda Wenman*

As CAT grew it got harder and harder to sustain its principles in a way that was entirely beneficial for the staff and for the smooth running of what had become a financially complicated business.

> "I think it's a shame at CAT, what I left with, is how badly people sometimes treat each other within organisations trying to create change; when things got difficult they struggled and they ended up treating each other badly within CAT and, to be honest, my first job at Shelter, people treated each other badly there too when things were difficult. My analogy was that when we were at CAT there was all this effort being put into these external technologies of solar panels and wind turbines and hydro and this kind of stuff, but the internal stuff, the head technology was being ignored. More and more what we recognise is that there's a technology inside our heads that is programmed in a certain way depending on our family background, our culture, our social groups. In terms of CAT it seemed to mean we were programmed to be very dependent, or that we're very independent, and our ability to be interdependent was weak – but key to successful working in a workers' co-op. We're not trained to be interdependent so

See Appendix B for photo captions

when you set up a co-op like CAT and you're basically saying, similar to the renewable energy, you're saying, 'We're going to find some different way of meeting our needs in terms of renewable energy', and when you set up a co-op you're going to say 'We're trying to find a different way to operate', but you don't consider that the operating system in our heads might need some tweaking, the same way renewable energy has needed to be developed and tweaked. Especially when you've got a bunch of people who are trying to save the world. People who have been forced to kind of look outside themselves have had to become headstrong and aren't always the best people to start working together, and no work was ever done on that brain technology, as it were, or the mind, or how we interrelated. But I do think that is changing now and most of my work now is on integrating psychology and the social sciences into this work, which is very exciting."

Rachel Lilley

There was a further complication, in that CAT was not set up as a workers' co-operative but as a charity (later a PLC was also established). Thus workers could not be members of an actual co-op but only participants in a flat management structure that we all called a co-op. It was thus possible for people to get the impression that they were joining a co-op and then find out that they weren't; well, not really. By the late 80s there was even confusion about whether, as a member of staff, you were a 'co-op member' or not. This was because, by then, staff were either appointed as 'Full Co-op Members', 'Associate Co-op Members', 'Casuals' or 'Volunteers' – depending on how much responsibility they had in their day-to-day job.

Full Co-op Members had the most responsibility, were expected to put themselves forward for election to Overview and could vote and attend and speak at meetings. Associate Co-op Members could not vote or stand for election to overview but could attend and speak at meetings. Casuals could not vote or attend meetings. Volunteers could attend some meetings but sometimes were not allowed to speak and were never enabled with a vote.

Not being able to vote was generally not a problem because voting was quite rare, and most decisions were talked out until consensus was reached. However it had the psychological effect of excluding valued members of staff from the decision-making process and making them feel like they were somehow less important.

Furthermore, from 2007 onwards – following the establishment of the Graduate School of the Environment – a group of academic staff employed by CAT on academic pay scales were also excluded from the co-op, leaving some of them feeling disenfranchised.

"[At that point] I'm based in the Eco park in Machynlleth, not at CAT, and we're denied any sort of co-operative membership status, so I have no part in CAT's politics or management. I feel very much like something separate … The staff at CAT were also going through their own crises and redundancies. They didn't have so much sympathy for people from the GSE who were earning more, but that rift was really unproductive. All those rifts needed resolving and didn't get resolved."

Kelvin Mason

Management reform at CAT

"When you've got 20, 30 or even 40 people there you can all sit around, discuss the issues and go away with a fairly common, reasonable understanding of what you all want to do. Once you're over 100 there's no way you can do that. You have a meeting with everybody there. Everybody thinks they understand what the outcome is but everyone has a different understanding of what the outcome is. And so you have to start putting in processes, procedures and policies so that everybody follows the rules. And it becomes less flexible, and it becomes easier for people who don't want things to change to keep things as they are. There is this thing called 'the tyranny of consensus', which favours the status quo. If you make a proposal it's very easy for people to block change. Much more difficult to get things to move forward, and you only need a very small number of people to block change."

Phil Horton

Between 1998 and 2010 CAT's turnover, staff body, legal responsibilities and debt had all increased substantially, creating a weighty rush of ever more complicated decisions that had to be taken by somebody. This included the management of the construction of the £6 million plus Wales Institute for Sustainable Education (WISE) – completed between 2002 and 2010 – a complex project involving multiple funding streams, building contractors and users.

Being on Overview was considered by many to be an arduous and unpleasant experience, and even though all permanent staff members were obliged to stand for election to the group, a substantial number of people felt unable to do so, for a wide variety of reasons. Those that did stand often had to give up the parts of their jobs they really enjoyed or take on an extra burden of work to make sure everything that needed to be done was done. They could also find themselves on the receiving end of some sharp-tongued criticisms from disgruntled fellow co-op members who suddenly saw them as 'the management'. Thick skins, if not already acquired, became an essential accessory.

When I was on Overview (for about seven months between 2003–2004), weekly meetings could last the whole day. During that day the group (made up of 5 elected members plus ex-officio representatives) could be asked to make decisions about a wide range of issues. For example: whether or not more money should be invested in fixing an ailing wind turbine; who should sit on a disciplinary panel; what budgetary targets should be set for the next year; who should become the latest site community resident, and so on.

There were only two qualifications required to be on Overview: one was to be a 'Full Co-op Member' (FCM) and the other was to be considered electable by your peers (although quite often candidates were 'elected' without opposition). Although Overview members (or reps as they were known) often had a great deal of experience, this also meant that someone with no line management experience, no financial management experience (apart from perhaps managing a small departmental budget) and no technical knowledge of the services about which they would make decisions could stand and be elected.

There was also no management training or induction process when joining Overview, so reps could be doing their normal job one day and be managing the company the next. Instead reps had to 'bed-in' over an 18-month term of office, gain experience as they went along and hope to be guided, at least at the beginning, by more experienced reps. I think it is fair to say that the experience of being an Overview rep was different for each person who took up the challenge and that the experience of being managed by Overview was different for each person. 'Overview' as an area of interest comes up in many of the interviews and the only way to get a range of opinions is to listen to them: those of Pete Raine, Roger Kelly, Louise Halestrap, Phil Horton, Andy Rowland, Annie Lowmass, James Cass and Tanya Hawkes are all good starting points.

"You were being voted on to what was essentially a board of directors and having to take on responsibility for various aspects of the organisation in two ways that seemed absurd. First of all people didn't necessarily have training for the specific legal responsibilities that they were having to take on, and although we were always enthusiastic and felt that we could do it and draw in the expertise when we needed it, it actually became very difficult to get people to stand for Overview. Because a lot of the time people had very full full-time jobs that they were having to do anyway, and suddenly you were being expected to invent a day and a half or two days' worth of extra time in an already very full week in order to be able to go on to Overview. So it did feel very much to me like we needed to have people who were working on this executive board that were paid, that they didn't have to, like me, go off and raise millions of pounds for WISE at the same time as spending a lot of time working through the board issues that there were. And also, of course, when you were on Overview you also had constituents. There were a whole group of people who were, if you like, your responsibility and you were supposed to look after these people, and any time they had any kind of issue or gripe at all they could come to you and you were expected to look after them. And to solve whatever it was that were the issues. And sometimes these issues were quite serious and sometimes they were the niggling, relatively trivial things. I very much felt that it was a bit of a daft situation that there was work for an executive board that needed to happen but that we hadn't got that. As the organisation was expanding I thought it was necessary that this board was created."

James Cass

"The check and balance was that I could have said, 'I don't think that's good enough, I'm going to resubmit that proposal', and it would have to be discussed again at Overview. If you submitted something three times and you weren't happy with the response it automatically had to go to a permanent staff meeting. So there was this interesting check and balance going on where literally any member of staff, no matter what department they were from or what their place was within the organisation, had this mechanism that they could use where they could get anything that needed discussing on the agenda for the permanent staff meeting, and I think it worked pretty well. When you say that to people they think, 'Oh my god so everyone was just discussing everything', but obviously they didn't, because usually most things that crop up would get resolved without going to a big meeting. But it just meant that if serious things didn't get resolved there was this mechanism to have it aired by the whole staff body. There were some people who felt very comfortable with the co-operative structure and consensus decision-making but some people either weren't comfortable with it, or even if they were, didn't really know the mechanisms available to them or how it all worked. Perhaps, on reflection, one of the drawbacks was the assumption that people understood it, and people not receiving training, particularly around how to engage with it, or how to use it, and I think it's probably a lesson for all kinds of flat-structure organisations that it's a danger if people don't feel like they're part of it, or have the opportunity to be part of it. There was always a stark difference between people whose jobs could be a bit more flexible [and those that weren't]. You could leave your day job to go into a meeting, whereas if you were someone who worked in the restaurant or in the shop it was very hard to leave what you were doing and be involved in the running of the organisation. It became really obvious that that was an inequality, in a way, in the structure."

Tanya Hawkes

The question of management reform vexed the organisation for many years – a management review group set up in the late 1990s to tackle perceived problems within the co-op management system really gained momentum between 2006 and 2010 – but the co-op was fundamentally split between those who wanted a lot of change, a little change or no change at all. The trustees also expressed disquiet that the co-op system was not capable of meeting the increased demands placed upon it.

Then, in 2010, the Overview group was replaced by a 'dual operating system' that included a Directions team and an Operations team. The Directions team was made up of elected members of staff, and the Operations team was made up of four hired 'civil servants' who were set the task of managing the day-to-day operations of CAT. This was the first collective acknowledgement that CAT needed to employ people who would just manage. These 'civil servants' would still be part of the co-op but their sole job would be to manage. This meant that they would not be responsible for running a department or project within CAT: a fundamental departure from the previous system.

This new system, designed by WISE project manager and former information officer Phil Horton, was a response to on-going concerns that Overview did not have the capacity to cope with CAT's rapid expansion. It was chosen in a ballot of all members of the 'co-op' (but not the Graduate School lecturers) after an extensive all-staff consultation, as the most favoured of four alternative operating systems proposed to replace Overview.

However, it proved very difficult to employ four experienced managers who were willing to work for CAT's below-industry-average wages. And although four candidates were selected, two of the managers left relatively quickly and it proved difficult to replace them.

By coincidence, around the same time it also became clear that the organisation was heading towards a cash flow crisis that, if left unchecked, would leave the organisation without the funds to pay its staff and thus to carry on its work. The trustees, with final legal responsibility, had to choose between closing CAT down and finding a way of carrying on. After taking legal advice they chose the latter and set in motion a strategic review to determine future operating arrangements for the organisation.

The trustees, working alongside the Directions team and Operations team, along with other members of staff and some key stakeholders, searched for an effective response to the crisis. What emerged from this process was a series of shock measures, given the context of CAT's history: the introduction of a hierarchical management structure, the appointment of a joint CEO/Finance Director and the decision to cut the wages bill through hours and staff reductions. There was also a proposal to seek a strategic partnership with a Welsh university. Interviewed in 2013, here are trustees Cynog Dafis and Iolo ap Gwynn.

"As a board we felt that the new management system, involving an Operations Team and a Directions Team, must be given the chance to prove itself. I hoped that it would lead to decision making and implementation being improved. With time it became clear that the new system was not effective enough. Also we knew that CAT had to face competition with other institutions that were offering some of the same courses and activities that had been unique to CAT. Since then we have moved to a more hierarchical management system, and there has been greater emphasis on financial management – much needed to keep CAT afloat. What we wanted was to have a management system that was efficient but which also respected CAT's special ethos. Personally I would like to see CAT linked more strongly to the Welsh HE system and to be more strongly rooted in the national life of Wales. That would in my view strengthen CAT, which in turn would enrich the Welsh HE system and give substance to the idea of making Wales an exemplar of sustainable development."

Cynog Dafis

"Of course there have been big changes over the last few years for the simple reason that the charity must not run on a loss. So we have had to make changes and have been trying for support from different directions for making these changes. The staff has been extremely, extremely good in the way that they have responded, and I believe that I have the feeling that many of the staff have realised that we have to change whatever, but the hope was of course when we're out of the present period, it would be possible to bring back many of the co-operative principles to run the centre. Eventually, isn't it."

Iolo ap Gwynn[1]

Whether the dual operating system of the Operations and Directions teams was the right one for CAT can be questioned because, in practical terms, it did not work. It was chosen in a collective, fair way by the required majority, after a very rigorous discussion process, but it failed to meet the financial challenges – which begs the question: can the decision to be managed this way be regarded as a collective failure?

Or was CAT just unlucky? This period of management change coincided with a number of severe economic shocks that put CAT under huge financial pressure. The recession, combined with changes in government policy on the environment and higher education funding, a drop in student numbers, and on-going disputes with the contractors employed to build WISE – which resulted in CAT being unable to access several hundred thousand pounds worth of compensation owed to it – created a perfect storm of prolonged disruption that would have severely tested any management structure and, indeed, the managers given the responsibility of making it work.

"From the very, very first day of my being at CAT as a staff member [in the Operations team role in charge of core services] it was all about 'Well, what are we going to do, how are we going to restructure? What are we going to do about saving huge amounts of money?' And again it felt like the universe dealing me a very nasty bad joke because it felt like, having wanted to be able to contribute to the kind of joy of the place, instead feeling like I was being asked to contribute to its slashing, and to hurting people, and it just was devastating, really, horrendous. It was way beyond my competence. It wasn't what I thought I'd be dealing with. I didn't have any experience or competence downsizing an organisation or dealing with a massive financial problem."

Sally Carr

---

[1] In 2014 CAT cemented its hierarchy with the appointment of a new CEO and a new layer of senior management.

"I guess management review at CAT has been going on for a long time because there was a management review group there when I started in 1998 and there was still one there when I left in 2010, but we went through a process which probably took two years from start to finish, going through that formal review process. What was agreed by everybody was that we needed to change the structure that we had. It was clear that people weren't able to do that Overview role in addition to their existing jobs. It just didn't work. It took up far too much time and it caused far too much stress for the people who were doing it. So the organisation did agree by consensus that we needed to have a new structure. A number of people put together four or five proposed new structures. Some of which were very similar to what we already had, some of which were radically different. We had a whole load of workshops, [after which we would] go away and rework our proposals to try and take account of what people were saying. I guess it was like an election campaign in some ways. We had hustings and quite vigorous debates, all of which was really important. I think nearly everybody in the organisation came along to a workshop or gave their written responses. We whittled it down to two proposals: my proposal and Ann's [education officer Ann MacGarry's]. Eventually we had a vote on it, which I think was done through a single transferable vote system, and so the system that I chose was selected and everybody got behind that. But we struggled to get people to apply because CAT salaries, as always, were pretty low (about £17,000), but we did find some suitable candidates. But, because effectively they came into a fire-fighting situation where we had all sorts of financial difficulties, really the structure never had a chance to get going properly. I supposed I would say this, but I still think it's a good structure. I think it should work, but it needs to be in a stable situation in the first place."

Phil Horton

Regrettably, these questions are too big to answer in full here but they are worth exploring because they ask us to think about co-operative and democratic values, the process of democratic change and co-operative governance. Many people are not served well by hierarchical systems, which is why it is important to find reliable, workable alternatives. With all its faults, the co-operative system allowed us to have a stake in the decision-making process and allowed us to choose the direction in which our own working lives travelled.

"You couldn't tell someone what to do and no one could tell you what to do, so some simple decisions meant that endless meetings and committees and groups were formed to finalise something that seemed so bloody simple in the first place. It's stressful but it was very good. If you were to say, 'Was that better than a hierarchical system?' I'd say yes every time, yeah every time yeah."

Rennie Telford

"The anecdotes I've told you today [are] splendid cannon fodder for anybody who wants to say, 'But that was absurd!' Yes it was absurd, I don't doubt it, but the experience of living through it wasn't. From a psychological point of view it gave the feeling that everybody was, er, to use a modern phrase, a stakeholder, in what we were doing. It kept everybody involved. It kept everybody feeling that they mattered, that they had some contribution to make."

John Urry

"It was a bit of a shock coming in [shortly after the dual operating system ended]. I had no idea about any of the problems CAT was having, at all, so I came in thinking everything was dandy. I was quite shocked to find out how negative people were and a bit down about it too, really. The re-structuring has definitely affected things. I'd love to see it go back to co-operative. I know that is part of the essence of CAT. That's something a lot of people find so negative, the fact that it is so hierarchical and it never was. There's not that element of communication these days. Before I started, there was monthly meetings and everyone who worked at CAT was in the know with what was going on, but now we don't have that.

Phoebe Gauntlett, speaking in January 2013

"The length of time that we were able to manage ourselves in a very co-operative manner with as fair elections as you could hope to get – and survive all that time – is something I feel very proud of. And although those things have changed now for financial reasons, it wasn't just a flash in the pan. For thirty years we managed ourselves and grew in that way so I do feel proud we were able to do that."

Annie Lowmass

"What has struck me most of all, despite all the problems, is that the dedication of the staff to CAT as an institution has remained. The Zero Carbon Britain research project has continued, and praise for CAT's courses is notable. What's needed now is to further develop the emphasis on business and effective management so that CAT can continue to lead the field and tell the truth about the state of the natural environment."

Cynog Dafis

The site community

It's not clear whether CAT was set up as intentional community or whether its community emerged from the practicalities of living and working on a quarry site with a number of serviceable cottages, and because accommodation and food could be offered in lieu of wages, given that there was not enough money to pay everyone for their labour. Gerard had visited many communities in America and had found some of them deeply unimpressive, disorganised and rapidly failing. He also had no intention of living in this kind of community, and indeed only ever stayed – rather than lived – at CAT.

"Once a plan has been decided, most people with a military background usually want to execute it with some degree of alacrity, and I think sometimes what frustrated him at the quarry were the type of debates that went on too long, often to agree something relatively straightforward. If he felt he could see a clear answer, he couldn't see why it required yet another debate. I suspect it might have driven him mad if he'd lived there on a full time basis and equally, he would probably have driven everyone there mad as well. He probably best served CAT by not being there on a full time basis."

George Morgan-Grenville

The on-site community is mentioned in the founding document but as a detached project separate to the rest of the quarry. This suggests that CAT was not set up as a kind of post-industrial, worker-controlled utopian village in the tradition of Robert Owen but as a scientific institute with a community on the side. There is no mention of co-operative values or even ideas of sharing resources through communal living. The main focus is on energy, re-cycling, building, food and transport.

"10. A subsequent project, now in the planning stages, concerns the establishment of an autonomous community where the results of the research at Llwyngwern can be applied in a practical form. The purpose of this will be not only to give those who wish to adapt their life-styles to such a form the opportunity to do so, but also to provide a demonstration of the relevance of such life-styles to any long-term reduction of environmental problems."

Nevertheless living 'on site' became, for many people, one of the main practical and philosophical attractions of coming to work at CAT. It became an immersive experience. The commute was abolished, home and work life became inseparable, food, energy and water a shared resource and the provision of all three a shared experience. Negotiating rota systems, cooking for tens of people, inviting strangers to the dinner table every day of the week, chopping wood, sharing food orders and child care: these and many other small details of communal living brought people out of their insular nuclear family backgrounds and allowed them to have shared experiences which were mostly, though inevitably not always, enriching.

"A big part of growing up at CAT was using the whole site as an adventure playground. Once the visitors went home the site was ours to do as we wish. We had treehouses, one over the bogerty bog, over the area where the waterwheel used to be. We used to do lots of tree climbing. Sunday was kiddies' games day where all the kids would get together. We had magicians and we'd do organised Easter egg hunts. When we were a bit older we took it in turns to cook for the community suppers and that really empowered us as kids; that gave us a sense of being more grown up and contributing to the community."

Cath McLennan

"For some years it was quite a vibrant group. It made for a lot of cohesion in the sense that you could continue meetings and discussions. It was a real think tank or encyclopaedia, really. There was a lot of people who knew lots of things. [It was] notoriously good for solving crossword clues because we had an intercom system, and you could broadcast and talk to anybody in their houses. So if you were stuck on a particularly challenging word you could call out and there would always be some smart devil who had the answer. There was always chemists and biochemists and architects and a whole range of serious knowledge. I quite liked that. I liked having lots of people around. Now that I'm retired I miss that occasionally. It's quite nice having a handy source of information, which I also had when I worked in industry. In a drawing office there were lots of highly skilled engineers. For mechanical things and stuff rather than ideas, there's an enormous wealth of knowledge there. You don't really realise what you've got until you haven't got it. How do I find this out now? Where do you go as an isolated private individual? This great enormous volume of knowledge and wisdom is lost to you unless you hang out in big offices or around big tables at some point of the day. So I quite liked that at CAT."

Clive Newman

Most importantly the on-site community also gave CAT the seal of authenticity, especially when it came to electricity generation, which was, for at least thirty years, entirely independent from the national grid.

Living an 'off-the-grid' lifestyle was certainly an attractive idea for many urban environmentalists seeking to escape reliance on nuclear power, but for some locals it was an unfathomable return to an intermittent way of life they had only recently given up – the first grid connection having arrived in the area in the 1960s. They couldn't understand why the new arrivals would want to give up so easily the idea that electricity was there whenever you wanted it. They knew full well that they were disadvantaged compared to the rest of the population. To them, off-the-grid living meant dependence on unpredictable weather conditions and technology.

"Electricity came to this area in 1961. Well, prior to that I had a water turbine and I was providing electricity for eleven different properties all 'round. When the water was short in the summer we had to have a stand by engine, and in the autumn the inherent problem was leaves blocking the sluices. And I remember once having to get up from the chapel in the middle of the service because the light was getting dim, and I had to go out and rake the leaves, and it was an excuse not to go back and listen to the sermon (laughs). All of a sudden we had electricity in '61, which was very cheap in those days, and of course these people come along and want to set up wind turbines and water turbines and I thought: 'What for, we've got cheap electricity at a constant supply.'"

Huw Jones

"Obviously there were times when there was no water, and no wind and no solar, and all we had left was the inverter, which was the battery system which stored everything. [Then] you were pretty much down to a light bulb each; you were just sitting around a 25-watt light bulb. You could also tell where the electricity was going. So you would stand in [the control room: 'Bob's Den'] and you would warn people that you were 'switching over to the inverter now so can everybody turn things off', and you could see people turning things off and the power demand going down, and then sometimes one part of the site would stubbornly stay up and you knew somebody was watching their TV. Sometimes you had to go and knock on the door …"

Lesley Bradnam

"Those turbines were a significant part of our lives at the time. They were producing some of our electricity. We used so little in the early days. I remember one night when there was a big storm, we were all sitting in Tim Kirby's house. Suddenly Tim Kirby realises that some of the sounds we can hear isn't the usual [sound] of the wind turbines but is the alarming clatter of the old Cretan actually starting to rip itself apart in the gale. So Tim, myself and one other just ended up running up the side of the slate waste in this gale with lashing rain, and furling its sails so it wouldn't destroy itself. Clearly as a guide to life in the 21st century we're not going to recommend that this is going to pull us out of the hole we're in, but as an experience for a young man it just lives in my memory of such a vivid thing and a reminder of how not to take electricity ever for granted."

John Urry

At CAT you could not bring power-hungry gadgets such as hairdryers on site (shocking to some visitors) and you could be asked to switch off your TV set halfway through the programme you were watching (by an engineer via what some might regard as a slightly Orwellian intercom system). This could cause griping, especially amongst families with children, but it did encourage socialisation, storytelling, conversation and a self-sufficiency of spirit.

"There was no radio up there, no television. Videos, CDs and DVDs didn't yet exist and thus the only form of entertainment was really people's voices and the odd guitar. We definitely sang a bit, but the overriding tendency was a lot of terrific conversation ranging from people telling funny anecdotes to hot debates on the subjects of the day. Everybody listened to everybody else's point of view, so I think my memories were [of] a really exceptional, interesting and diverse bunch of people up there."

George Morgan-Grenville

It also taught everyone who encountered it the value of having just a few watts of power, something which could give you a great deal of empathy with the vast majority of the world who don't have access to any electricity.

"Everybody had a couple of hundred watts to play with. You learnt the value of the fact that it was those first few hundred watts that changed your life, because they're the ones that enabled you to have light at night, enabled you to run electronics and I guess computers ... and we could run one communal fridge."

Pete Raine

This Desirable Residence

Cottage 4, on site.
Rent: an astonishing
£21 a week!

From now onward.

Features :

* *En suite* bathroom
* Solar Panels!
* Both internal *and* external wall insulation.
* Baby belling oven, 2 gas rings and grill.
* Feisty Little Wenlock stove, burns wood or coal. Could be replaced with a woodburner.
* Spacious bed platform.
* Ethnic stable door
* Spacious new compost loo next door.
* Highly convenient for nearby dump, the famous "Cleavage"
* Some furnishings included.

Any CAT employees interested, please contact John Urry.

See Appendix B for photo captions

Electricity suddenly became a precious resource, to be saved and used as effectively as possible by the whole community. You had to think about your neighbours' needs as well as your own. If someone wanted to put the washing machine on, other things had to be turned off.

This was a lesson eventually passed on to successive groups of school children staying in CAT's Eco-cabins, which are still very much modelled on the same principles of shared living experiences. Children arrive at the start of the week with a full battery store of electricity but have to be careful how much they use because the store can only be replenished if weather conditions allow it, although it should be added that the children are never left to go without, and the system is now connected to a micro-grid for the whole site.

"When groups come to the cabins they have an all-encompassing educational experience. We have a lot of city children come who have never seen a tomato on a plant or they've never seen a sheep, and so as well as teaching them about renewable energy we take them up in the hills, and they're completely gobsmacked that there's poo on the ground that sheep have made. [When the Eco-cabins were set up] we got schools to book five years' worth of timeshares, which brought the money up front and helped build the cabins. And then the schools had a set programme and they came for five years, and after that scheme had finished we didn't know whether they would carry on coming but they did. They carried on coming year after year, and they continued to do so. It's such a unique experience that schools come back continuously. It was a great idea. It wasn't my idea. I wish I could claim ownership of that but, because we could see it as a really fantastic experience to have them actually living and doing it, because they have to manage their power. There's a battery system down at the cabins that is their reservoir of power. They have that power to start with and they mustn't run out of power. They can see, they've got a special monitoring board. It teaches them to turn lights off, and that they can't use things like hairdryers whilst they're in the cabins. It sounds quite brutal but in fact they love it. It really teaches them about energy and looking after it. They

have competitions, one cabin with another; if they're in the
same school and they're in two cabins, they'll compete with
each other to see how much power they've each got."

Christine McLennan

Arrivals

"We had a book called *The Rural Resettlement Hand-book*, which
was to give you advice and guidance on how to move out of
towns, so you had a map of Britain and you drew 'round all
the towns and you drew 'round all the airfields, the RAF bases,
and you drew a border 'round Britain five miles inland, cos it's
always more expensive on the coast, and then you see what's
left, (laughs) and so of course a lot of Wales was left."

Sabrina Cantor

On February 2nd 2014 we celebrated the 40th anniversary of the
arrival of the first person to come to work at CAT – Tony Williams.
We know the exact date work started – February 2nd 1974 – because
a diary was kept throughout the whole of the first year in which
progress, setbacks, squabbles, philosophical discussions, visitors and,
not least of all, the weather are recorded.

Tony Williams kept the diary for two months, and then left CAT
mysteriously. We're not exactly sure why because we haven't been able
to track him down for an interview yet, but there are several references
in the diary to frustrating arguments and exhaustion. One of his diary
entries ominously states: "Learning to live with people is harder than
to learn to live without them." Another shows that he, and perhaps
the whole group, had failed to master the basic concept of a weekend:
"After six weeks of uninterrupted work I decided to take a day off. I
ought to program a system of days off."

Arriving at CAT is part of the mythology of the place. Everyone has
their own arrival story. Because of where it is, most people have already
taken a journey to get there – to leave behind the world they know
and start on a new adventure. Then, once you arrive, you also have to
climb to get to the site, up a steep track under a canopy of trees.

There is something about this climb that is both mysterious and exciting. It is long enough to give you time to think about what experience you might be about to have when you arrive at the top and pretty enough to feel as though you have already been seduced by the atmosphere of the place when you get there. Even if you arrive in heavy rain – as many people have over the years – the scene can be, at the very least, dramatic, as streams of running water form and cascade down towards you.

"It was January the fifteenth I ended up going up there and um – it was a really wet horrible old day, and I think it was about four o'clock. It was pretty dark as well and I made my way up what appeared to be the path. But it seemed more like a river bed, and I got two thirds of the way up and then decided: 'No, I'm going to come back down again.' It was when I got to the bottom, I spotted a couple of pints of milk – that were hidden at the bottom of the path – and decided, well, it must be the way forward, so I went back up to the top, and eventually when I got to the top found this old tumbledown building with a plastic sheet over the top. By this time it really was nearly dark, and I ventured through this gap in the wall, and there was a couple of benches in there with a couple of plates where obviously somebody had had some food there, and a Jøtul stove, which was going, and I could just see a shadowy figure in the background. That was Bob Ashcroft. A chap who arrived the next day had a smock and a sailor's hat, and this was Richard St George, and the two of us were thrown together into one room in one of the derelict cottages [to sleep], and he became a lifelong friend. He had a public school background, I came from a secondary school but we got on and we had some great times together."

Des Rees, arriving from South Wales in 1975

"It was February, it was grey, it was wet and it was co-o-o-ld, um so I thought: 'Well, if I like it today I'll probably like it, whatever the weather.' [The people] were nice, jolly, quite cuddly, literally and metaphorically, um, and very approachable, and not quite as hippy as I think my father, who'd had to drop me off, had been imagining."

Caroline Oakley, arriving from London in 1998

The act of arriving at CAT is a commitment in itself. For many years, before CAT's modern education facility, WISE, was built, you had to be the kind of person who could enjoy rough and ready living. Just coming for an interview could be a culture shock.

"My first experience of CAT was turning up with a portfolio, and I'd dressed myself up. I'd put on my best clothes, shaved and splashed on the Old Spice. I walked into what was the restaurant, and in those days it was a shop too. The first person I met was Diana Francis, she was one of the chief cooks. My very first conversation went something like this: I said, 'I've got an appointment with Pete Raine', to which she replied in a really loud voice, 'You needn't have put that on to come here', followed by a hearty belly-laugh. I wasn't sure whether she was referring to the aftershave or my choice of clothing; probably both. I immediately felt quite out of place. She then said, 'I'll just get someone who'll take you along.' Next thing, in walked Felicity Shooter, dressed in dungarees and sporting an oversize pair of glasses, who then proceeded to march me down the railway track into this valley, passing all these little dilapidated slate buildings, finally arriving at Pete Raine's 'cottage' where I was ushered in. I remember thinking to myself 'What have I got myself into here?' This was the second meeting with Pete Raine, and the first time I met John Urry, who was sitting there with him. John and I went on to become work colleagues and the best of friends. John and Pete interviewed me and looked through my work; it was quite daunting. Anyway, they seemed happy enough. Pete Raine then asked me if I would be interested coming up to CAT as a 'vol' for a week. I remember having to ask: 'A 'vol' – what d'you mean, 'vol'?' 'A volunteer', he said; 'Ohhh right, yeah, OK.' Words like 'vol' have remained common parlance in the CAT vocabulary to this day, but at the time I didn't have a clue what he meant. The idea was, I was to go up to CAT to work voluntarily for a week, where we would mutually get to know one another, see how it worked out, on both sides. It was most definitely a type of screening process that went on in that week; a chance for the rest of the community to get to know you – 'Yeah, he's a nice fella, he'll fit in', kind of thing. I did my voluntary week and it was wonderful, what I can remember of it! And the rest of it, as they say, is history."

Graham Preston, arriving from Machynlleth in the mid 1980s

For many years part of the interview process included sharing lunch with the staff in the small staff house known as Tea Chest. Lunch times were generally very busy and, on a rainy day, very cosy. For as long as I can remember the same two large, rough, handmade wooden tables and four benches have accommodated the elbows and bottoms of the staff at CAT, and the experience is either intimate or intimidating depending on what kind of person you are. It's communal living; don't expect your own chair!

Well, there are plenty of stories of people turning up for the lunch and not staying for the interview, or volunteers turning up one day only to leave the next. You had to feel comfortable and at home with this way of living, or at the very least want to put up with it or adapt to it. But for some people who looked like they might not last the week, their first day at CAT was also a turning point.

"I turned up in immaculate clothes – brand new jeans and a bright white shirt – greeted by Sally Carr, who's now one of my best friends in the whole world. She was coordinating all the short term volunteers, and to this day she just still remembers looking at me and going: 'This is going to be interesting; how is this girl going to cope?' and Roger [McLennan, the gardener] took one look at me and thought exactly the same thing and thought: 'Right I'm going to put her to the test.' And so my first job was to go into the compost pit with a fork. The smell seeped into your clothes and skin after 5 minutes of being in there. It was rancid, just the most repugnant smell on earth. I had to go into this room and turn the compost, which was full of rats, and I remember just like being: 'No I'm going to do this', and Roger was next to me waiting for me to scream and run a mile, and [he] stabbed a rat with a fork right next to me, and I was still there, and I was still turning the compost, and I came out a different woman (laughs). A stinky one. And I had to wash that shirt so many times. But it was brilliant. It was horrific but was absolutely brilliant because I realised what I was capable of."

Thea Platt, arriving from Berkshire in 2002

Receive and Return

Christine Mills and Carlos Pinatti – two of our artists in residence – created an art piece based around themes of co-operation during their three-month residency at CAT. They organised a three-day workshop in which they worked with students and staff to create a tiled map of the world.

Inspired by students of the Graduate School playing Ping Pong in between lectures, Christine and Carlos then printed a digital image of the finished map in vinyl and overlaid it onto a Ping Pong table. In line with their original idea to give the piece a universal language by using no words, only symbols, they opted to accompany the Ping Pong table with a very simple video of an egg timer being turned over. Whilst watching the sands of time running out, the viewer listens to a surround-sound playback of water and Ping Pong balls.

This intensifies the experience of playing the game, suggesting that time is running out. The purpose of the Ping Pong game is not to win but to keep the ball on the table. The players are invited to move around the table helping each other to keep playing. Finally, underneath the table, is a blanket made from felted wool, gathered from the fields of local sheep farmer Ed Breese. The blanket represents the bed of Diana Brass, who used to sleep under her cook's table at CAT.

Chapter 4

Environmental quest
and technical endeavour

"We've never been too bothered about the idea that they've tried this and it didn't work," CAT member John Compton reassured me when I interviewed him and his wife Ann during a members' conference. "Somebody's got to try these things. Somebody's got to learn the lessons. If you don't risk failure you can't succeed."

In the nicest possible way, CAT was set up to fail. Its purpose was to test technology, see if it worked, and tell other people about it. The only two rules were to learn from failure and create change.

Taking the theme of failure as a starting point for investigating the technical and environmental achievements of CAT in its first 40 years may seem a little quirky, but it's important to contextualise what we did – and to count the ability to fail as a success in its own right. It gave all of us associated with the work that CAT did (members, workers, visitors) the freedom to engage a collective enquiring mind and apply it to all strands of CAT's work: the co-operative work structure, the site community, our educational pedagogy, the big projects, the day-to-day work, the research experiments, and so on.

This idea of principled evolutionary failure cropped up in many of the interviews, perhaps no more so than when I talked to CAT's professor of architecture Pat Borer and early pioneer, architect and CAT member Jane Bryant. Pat talked me through an experiment with an early solar air heater, which for many years lulled at less than optimum performance on the outside wall of cottage 2; Jane described CAT's experimental fish farm, which was supposed to cycle fish waste into plant nutrients to grow vegetables.

"It worked for a bit but it was another grand failure, of the 'failure is the compost of success' type, because that's why we did things: to see if they would work, because nobody anywhere was doing that and still don't."

Pat Borer

"The water never seemed to be at the temperature it was supposed to be at. Bob Todd helped me work out the area of solar panels we would need to get it up to a certain temperature; we did that but it never did. We estimated how much effluence would come out of the pond to feed the vegetables, but they never really grew. It was really miserable, looking at these beds of slate with nothing growing, with a windmill pumping fish waste 'round. It was hopeless. Nothing really worked in the early days except the community and the vibe."

Jane Bryant

You could apply this lens of principled evolutionary failure to many threads of CAT's work and look for the progression within it. Take for example wind power.

The first wind turbines at CAT were very primitive home-made machines such as the Cretan sail turbine (which produced a few watts of electricity but necessitated a great burning of calories as its human keepers clambered up and down the slate quarry to furl and unfurl its sails as the wind speed rose and fell); or small manufactured machines that were often old designs but were nevertheless tried and tested, such as the Winco (a 1940s turbine whose blade tips eventually burnt in action when the brake failed).

Bob Todd deserves much of the credit for establishing CAT's technological reputation. As well as establishing a site-wide electrical system to harness these idiosyncratic power sources, he created numerous inventions that have since been used around the world.

"There were a few people trying to make bigger, up to a kilowatt-scale wind turbines, and they were very unreliable and quickly fell apart or needed a lot of modifications. [The manufacturers of one turbine] sounded a little bit surprised that we were expecting it to generate power because the only other ones they had turning had been motored to show people what they would look like when they were running. In terms of energy production it was a disaster, but we did learn quite a lot from it. And there were quite a lot of other people in Britain who were interested, who came and crawled all over it and went away to do something better."

Bob Todd

Bob quickly realised that CAT needed to develop its own wind turbine components to enable greater control and thus better efficiencies, so he created automated system controllers that could react to weather conditions. These kinds of development later led to the creation of 'wind to heat' systems – that could dump energy into heating systems – and also, very importantly, greater understanding about what the manufacturers of wind turbines promised for their machines, compared to what they actually delivered.

During this evolutionary phase Roger White also created CAT's 'own-brand' wind turbine – the Aerotron, whose space-age name seems an ironic compliment to its home-made wooden blades and forged motor case made of recycled aluminium from melted-down gearboxes.

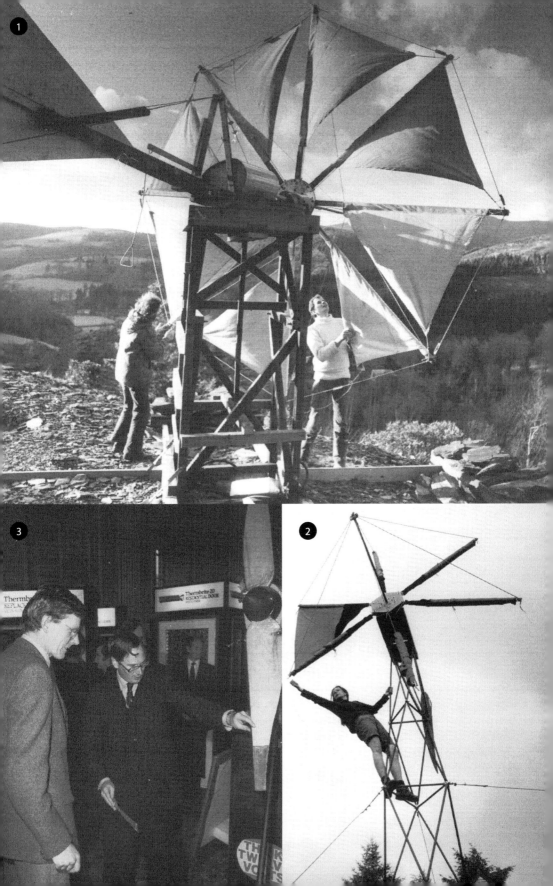

See Appendix B for photo captions

"They talked about building a huge great big Cretan Windmill. I said 'No, for goodness sake who's going to look after it, you're not sailing a boat on a Sunday afternoon.' You've got to have a horizontal axis with an aircraft blade. So I built this thing called the Aerotron, which had a cast body and essentially was a test bed that would stand a high wind and probably high rotational speeds. But as a generator unit I wanted to use something that was available worldwide and standard. So I thought: 'Let's see if I can lick an alternator into shape.' It was obviously going to be short lived but we did learn some very interesting things from it." (So much so that a later version of the Aerotron made it to the Antarctic with polar explorer Robert Swan, generating 300 watts 'at saturation' and surviving 120 miles per hour wind speeds).

Roger White

As time went on, these early technological explorations not only helped create change in the technology but also fed back into changes in the philosophy of CAT. In the early days CAT was portrayed by the media as a back-to-the land 'good life' experiment – not surprisingly, considering TV's similarly-themed sit com *The Good Life* was first broadcast in April 1975, only two months before CAT opened its doors as a visitor centre.

But Peter Harper, who coined the phrase 'alternative technology', recalls that there were dozens of ideas about what CAT was and should be, and believes one idea prevailed in the early days, which related to another TV programme broadcast in 1975: *Survivors*.

"Among the very many ideas about what it could be, was, as an experimental 'refugium', like the monks of Lindisfarne kept the manuscripts alive during the Dark Ages. At that time there was very widespread apocalyptic feeling about imminent collapse because of nuclear war or ecological collapse. Under those circumstances, what do you do? You might well start a place that knows how to rebuild after a collapse, taking nothing for granted. If there is a collapse, what do you need? You need centres where the skills are preserved; [centres that know] how to rebuild on the basis of very little, very simple principles and technologies. So that was what was favoured all the time: keep it simple, try to use basic materials. Things you can make yourself or scavenge. It was kind of refugee camp technology, or post-holocaust."

Peter Harper

Environmentalism and popular culture in the early 70s

Environmental concerns and energy security were big issues in 1973, thanks to a series of economic failures and strikes, a catastrophic rise in the price of oil and the publication of ground-breaking reports like *The Ecologist's Blueprint for Survival*. Even TV's *Dr Who* covered the subject in *The Green Death*. Broadcast in the summer of 1973, *The Green Death* sees the Doctor and his assistant Jo tackling toxic slime and giant maggots created by a multinational corporation run by a super computer indifferent to ecological damage and human life. Strangely the episode is set in a disused quarry in Wales and features Professor Jones, a fictional Nobel Prize winning biologist living in a commune called Wholeweal, whose work includes the creation of a fungus substitute for meat. As author Dominic Sandbrook recalls in his book *State of Emergency*: "In a clear victory for the forces of environmentalism it is precisely this fungus that kills the toxic slime." As the story comes to an end, "capitalism, chemicals and computers have been defeated . . . and the Doctor drives off disconsolately into the night, alone with only the memory of a hearty fungus meal to console him". (*State of Emergency, The Way We Were: Britain 1970–1974*, Dominic Sandbrook).

These *Good Life* and *Survivors* interpretations of CAT made it what it was, but also held it back. The arrival of this new phrase 'the good life' into popular culture probably helped cement affection for CAT in the public mind and sympathy for the comedic, heroic struggle of the people at CAT, who were perceived to be real-life Toms and Barbaras (the two struggling heroes of the show), working and living against the odds with next to nothing. But it also led to a misrepresentation of what CAT stood for, and threatened to pigeonhole it.

An Alternative
Energy Strategy
for the
United Kingdom

Centre for Alternative Technology

MAKING COMPOST

See Appendix B for photo captions

Furthermore the 'Refugium' notion meant that CAT struggled to move beyond its origins, to reach out to different audiences and integrate alternative technology into national thinking, despite projects such as 1977's *An Alternative Energy Strategy for the UK*. A lack of resources also meant that CAT was always in danger of being left behind, of accepting low wages as a price to pay for ethics, and of losing talented workers who could not afford to stay – or even begin.

An edgy tension evolved between those who wanted to keep it simple and those who strained to push CAT on towards the mainstream, a move that would effectively mean compromising the belief that the apocalypse was indeed imminent. Even the term 'alternative technology' was felt to be a millstone, with its suggestion of being on the fringe. The more CAT stayed with its small-scale technologies and 'small is survival' ethos, the more people were able to say that alternative technology was good to have in reserve but would never deliver anything substantial in the real economy.

So wind power at CAT evolved and moved outwards. Tim Kirby took CAT's energy production off site to a neighbouring farm, with the 15 kW Polenko turbine – probably one of the first farm-scale wind energy contracts negotiated in the UK. Next came the experimental wind-farm sized MS4-600 (brought to CAT by Clive Newman and Rob Gwillim), which also finally allowed CAT to philosophically and technologically connect with the rest of the world via the national grid.

Then came the development of the community windfarm, full connection to the grid and a market economy – buying and selling electricity from and to the grid as supply and demand fluctuated. As a spin-off, local farmer and engineer Edward Jones, who lifted the Polenko wind-turbine into place and helped construct the cliff railway and many other CAT engineering projects, built what was at the time Europe's largest windfarm on his own land, just down the valley from CAT at Cemmaes.

CAT could thus show that novel forms of renewable energy were capable of contributing meaningful amounts of electricity in real-world situations, finally pushing away from its own 'good life' iconography. Tom and Barbara took three years to abandon their idea. CAT took a lot longer, the final symbolic death knell perhaps coming in 2001 when CAT could no longer keep pigs because of legislation designed to halt the spread of foot and mouth disease.

"People had come up with all sorts of self-sufficiency models for how to do things, and we liked that idea. Right now I think that this is the worst idea. I'm really against it now. But at the time the idea was: if every little unit is self-sufficient and there's not a lot of trading then they've all got to add up to a sustainable thing, because they've all got to take responsibility for their own little bit. As soon as you're [trading globally] you're constantly trying to shift the costs on to someone else, so we thought this is a good decentralised model; that's largely where the idea of alternative technology came from."

Peter Harper

CAT's Zero Carbon Britain project – developed by project co-ordinator Paul Allen over a ten-year period – is the embodiment of this change in philosophy. It puts forward a plan that radically changes the way we use land in Britain and the way we generate and use energy. It also ties land use and energy production directly together so the plan only works if you change everything.

It is the sort of plan that can only be instigated by national government, with the support of citizens and business, as part of a global solution. It's ambitious in many ways, not least of all in that it requires decisions based on scientific fact rather than political expediency. And it relies not on self-sufficiency but on a hyper-organised energy grid that crosses continents and removes the variability issues that made localised, self-sufficient, off-grid living at CAT, whilst life-enhancing in some ways, so problematic.

"It was sort of in the back of my mind: how does all this stuff that CAT's going on about clip together to produce something that saves the world? If it all happened would that actually save the world or not? So one lunchtime, in a caffeine-fuelled frenzied lunch with two friends – Tim Helweg-Larsen and Sara Turnbull – we all said, 'Let's do it, let's re-do the Alternative Energy Strategy.' This was about 2005 so it was about twenty-odd years after it came out: 'Let's re-do it and see where we are.' We had no money whatsoever. We began with students' voluntary time and half a day a week of my time ... [Since then] we [have] managed to find the resources to put CAT back on the map of radical thinking rather than it being somewhat a nice sort of cosy place like it was in the 80s. So now we've got a new research team in place because things change. Energy technologies change. Understandings of climate change. Our report produced in 2010 doesn't have currency in 2013. We need a bang up-to-date report. So, on the strengths of the work so far, we've raised enough money to recruit a research team. We've got seven now working on it, including interns who've come from other European countries who want to work on it to get the experience to go and start similar projects in their own country."

Paul Allen, speaking in 2013

There has been one more change CAT has had to embrace: an acceptance that climate change is so far advanced that it is too late to rely only on technologies and practices that mitigate it. What we have to do now is try to stop the worst impacts of climate change with the mitigation technologies and practices CAT has always believed in, but at the same time explore ways that society might need to adapt in the face of changing global weather patterns – without increasing greenhouse gas emissions. In 2014 this shift was cemented by the creation at CAT of one of the UK's first MSc courses on Sustainability and Adaptation.

"There has always been a bit of me that had rather hoped that the green movement had got it wrong. It would be embarrassing that you had given your life's working to something that was barking up the wrong tree. Nonetheless I would have been very happy if they'd suddenly turned 'round and said, 'Look, you've got it all wrong; we've found this amazing clean source of energy that had sorted everything out', and we could have just walked away. The vindication that came in, and that is definitely there, I thought it was going to feel sweeter than it actually felt. The problem is it came so late and the problems are so great it doesn't feel as sweet as I'd hoped."

Rick Dance

ZERO CARBON BRITAIN

Science says we must
Technology says we can
Time to say we will

Rethinking the Future

Appendix A

Quote references

Paul Allen started at CAT as an engineering volunteer before going to work for Dulas Engineering. He returned to CAT as media officer before becoming director. He then went on to establish the Zero Carbon Britain project.

Bethan Bennett worked in several roles in CAT's mail order department, including as marketing manager.

Donald Bennett is the father of Bethan Bennett. He moved from South Wales to set up a pottery in the 1970s. In the early 2010s he worked at CAT as a caretaker in WISE.

Mark Bloomfield was a long term volunteer in the engineering department in the 2000s.

Pat Borer started at CAT as an architect, builder and graphic designer. He went on to co-author with Cindy Harris *The Whole House Book* and *Out of the Woods,* and with David Lea designed the AtEIC and WISE buildings. He is now visiting professor on CAT's Professional Diploma in Architecture course.

Lesley Bradnam was residential courses co-ordinator and information and consultancy co-ordinator. She was also a member of site community.

Julie Bromilow was a CAT bookshop assistant, a CAT information volunteer, an environmental education officer, and had undertaken research into the 'Decade of Education for Sustainable Development in Japan' before returning to CAT as an education officer from 2007–2012.

Architect **Jane Bryant** worked at CAT in the mid-1970s and is still a member.

Sabrina Cantor was Buy Green by Mail co-ordinator for over 20 years.

Sally Carr co-ordinated CAT's short term volunteer programme for many years, as a volunteer herself. She became an Operations team manager with responsibility for core services and now works in the fundraising department.

James Cass was a fundraiser at CAT and worked alongside Tanya Hawkes (below) and other staff members for several years. They were both involved with many of CAT's key fundraising campaigns, including WISE.

Cynog Dafis was an MP and Welsh Assembly Member and has been a trustee at CAT for many years. His interview was conducted in Welsh and transcribed and translated by Sarah Vaughan.

Rick Dance was volunteer and site community member 1983 to 1985; administrator at UCAT, Bristol (CAT's sister project, the Urban Centre for Alternative Technology) 1985 to 1987; office administrator at CAT 1987 to 1995; CAT company secretary, 1995 to 2015.

Janet Davies had two children, Fred and Kirsty. They are both successful artists.

Nigel Dudley was CAT's first education officer. He also worked in the Quarry Café.

Irene Galant came to CAT in 1977 to work as a secretary but then found herself working on other projects, including the bookshop, which led her subsequently to become involved in setting up Green Leaf Bookshop in Bristol. She is the mother of Suzanne Galant (not interviewed) who later co-authored CAT's *Little Book of Slugs*.

Phoebe Gauntlett worked as a student support officer for the Graduate School of the Environment for a few months in 2013, shortly after the co-op system had been disbanded.

George Morgan-Grenville is the son of CAT's founder Gerard Morgan-Grenville. He visited CAT for a holiday in the 1970s.

Jo Gwillim worked as an engineer for Dulas Engineering before coming back to work many years later as an education officer.

Iolo ap Gwynn was a trustee for over twenty years and Chair for several years. His interview was conducted in Welsh and transcribed and translated by Sarah Vaughan.

Louise Halestrap was CAT's biologist for several years, later returning as a lecturer in the Graduate School of the Environment.

Peter Harper came to CAT as a landscape co-ordinator but worked in various positions, as described on page 16.

Tanya Hawkes was a fundraiser at CAT, working alongside James Cass (above). She was also a member of site community and is now partner to Alex Randall. We interviewed Alex and Tanya separately and together.

Patrick Hannay was building editor of the UK's weekly *Architects Journal* for 13 years, and then ran the BA Interior Architecture degree course at UWIC Cardiff up to 2011. During that time he founded and edited *Touchstone,* the magazine for Architecture in Wales. He is currently a part time lecturer on CAT's Professional Diploma in Architecture.

Cindy Harris was CAT's builder for 17 years, managed build projects such as the Eco-cabins, the top station of the cliff railway and AtEIC, and led many short courses teaching timber frame self build methods, including those created by Walter Segal. She also co-authored with Pat Borer *Out of the Woods* and *The Whole House Book.*

Phil Horton joined CAT in 1998 as technical information officer. He went on to manage the construction project for the Wales Institute for Sustainable Education (WISE). He left CAT in 2011 to join CAT's spin-off renewables company Dulas.

Rod James was CAT's second director (1975–1980). You can hear Rod talking about his experiences at CAT on Radio 4's The Reunion on http://www.bbc.co.uk/programmes/b01s393k and in Glenn Davidson's sonic poem at http://www.artstation.org.uk/CAT/CAT.html

Edward Jones is a farmer and engineer. He also set up the Cemmaes wind farm and was contracted by CAT to help deliver several important engineering projects.

Huw Jones is a local farmer (still, in his 80s). He was a local councillor when CAT was seeking approval to start, and later supplied CAT with cut timber from his sawmill.

Kit Jones works in CAT's media department.

Tobi Kellner was CAT's information officer before becoming a consultant and lecturer and then working on the Zero Carbon Britain project as an energy modeller.

Roger Kelly was CAT's fourth director, between 1988 and 1998. He was also a member of site community.

Gayle Light is married to Jeremy Light and mother of Angus, Gemma and Alice (see below). She is also a concert pianist and piano teacher.

Jeremy Light was CAT's ecological director in the 70s and 80s, working on various projects including developing the reed bed sewage system. He is husband to Gayle Light and father to Angus and Gemma (both interviewed) and Alice (not yet interviewed).

Rachel Lilley was CAT's development co-ordinator for several years and worked primarily on the AtEIC fundraising campaign.

Annie Lowmass was the co-ordinator of the Quarry Shop and Cafe for many years from the early 1980s, before taking up a position at CAT as Ecostore and visitor centre manager. Her husband Michael Tomlinson (not yet interviewed) also managed the Quarry Shop and Cafe as well as the CAT Restaurant – and is an artist.

Ann MacGarry is an education officer. She has worked at CAT since 1989.

Kelvin Mason had two periods working at CAT, separated by a long absence. Most recently he helped to develop the distance learning programme in the GSE.

Mark Mathews was co-director with his then wife Mary Mathews in 1974. They worked at CAT for a few months during that difficult first year. You can hear Mark talking about his experiences at CAT on Radio 4's The Reunion on http://www.bbc.co.uk/programmes/b01s393k and in Glenn Davidson's sonic poem at http://www.artstation.org.uk/CAT/CAT.html

Catherine McLennan is daughter to Roger and Christine and grew up on site. She later went on to work in the fundraising department.

Christine McLennan has been an education officer for many years, working primarily with children visiting the Eco-cabins. She also toured in a 'theatre in education' company and wrote a play performed as part of CAT's children's activities. She is married to Roger McLennan.

Roger McLennan has worked as CAT's gardener and head gardener since 1978. He is married to one of CAT's education officers, Christine McLennan. Their daughter Catherine has also been interviewed.

Megan Mills was a 'Quarry kid', daughter of engineer Nick Mills (also interviewed), and worked in CAT's information department and in the Quarry Café.

Clive Newman was CAT's engineer for many years. His large projects included the cliff railway and the MS4-600 community wind turbine, but he was also responsible for many others. He was a member of site community most of that time.

Sally Oakes worked in the information department in the 2000s. Sally is married to Jake Voelcker (see 6 below). We interviewed Jake and Sally together.

Caroline Oakley was CAT's publisher for over a decade. She also co-authored *52 Weeks to Change Your World*.

Hele Oakley worked in CAT's publications department in the 2000s. She has also worked as freelance editor on several CAT books, including *Zero Carbon Britain 2030*.

Chris Parrott has for many years worked on CAT's cliff railway as an operator, also assisting with maintenance and engineering tasks.

Thea Platt came as a short term volunteer in the early 2000s before working in CAT's media department as a long term volunteer.

Graham Preston worked alongside John Urry as an illustrator and graphic designer for many years before working as a production designer for CAT's publications department for approximately twenty years.

Pete Raine was CAT's director between 1980 and 1986.

Alex Randall worked primarily in the media and fundraising departments. He is partner to Tanya Hawkes.

Joan Randle started at CAT as an education officer in a job share with her husband Damian Randle. Joan went on to become short courses co-ordinator before co-founding and managing the Graduate School of the Environment. With Pat Borer, she was also the originator of the WISE project.

Delyth Rees taught Welsh at CAT and later became a CAT trustee.

Des Rees worked at CAT for a short period in the 1970s on various projects. You can hear Des talking about his experiences at CAT on Radio 4's The Reunion on http://www.bbc.co.uk/programmes/ b01s393k

Andy Rowland managed the visitor centre for many years at CAT before leaving to manage Ecodyfi, a local community project.

Rebecca Sullivan works in CAT's membership department.

Rennie Telford was the Eco-cabins maintenance officer. He also wrote a regular all-staff email called Naycher Korner, which contained many amusing anecdotes about wildlife, many of which concerned sightings at CAT.

Judith Thornton started as a maintenance volunteer at CAT before going on to work in the biology office and then later becoming a lecturer in the Graduate School of the Environment.

Bob Todd was CAT's technical director in the 70s and 80s before leaving to set up Aber Instruments. He is married to Liz Todd. You can hear Bob talking about his experiences at CAT on Radio 4's The Reunion on http://www.bbc.co.uk/programmes/b01s393k and in Glenn Davidson's sonic poem at http://www.artstation.org.uk/CAT/ CAT.html

Liz Todd is married to Bob Todd, technical director of CAT in the 1970s and 80s. She arrived at CAT with two year old James and very young baby Julie and lived on site to begin with. She later became a CAT trustee. You can hear Liz talking about her experiences at CAT on Radio 4's The Reunion on http://www.bbc.co.uk/programmes/ b01s393k

John Urry arrived in 1982 as a student to complete a university project but decided to stay and has been there ever since, most of that time as an illustrator and graphic designer. He has also been a member of site community since 1982 and is partner to Fiona Rowe (co-author of *The Sustainable Careers Handbook*) and father to Lexi (neither of whom have been interviewed).

Judith Varley has been a member of CAT for many years, having first visited CAT in the early 1970s.

Chloe Ward was a long term volunteer and forest gardener, later becoming CAT's displays gardener. She is also a lecturer, author of *How to Prune an Apple Tree* and co-author with Allan Shepherd of *The Organic Garden*.

Lynda Wenman worked in the Quarry Café for many years as a CAT employee and now manages it as a private business.

Roger White set up a forge at CAT in the late 1970s as well as creating the Aerotron wind turbine, amongst other projects. He later went on to do a substantial amount of the engineering work on the cliff railway.

Jill Whitehead worked at CAT in the 1970s. She is still a trustee of the Society for Environmental Improvement, the charity that set up CAT.

Jake Voelcker worked in the media department in the 2000s.

Appendix B

Photographic references

The CAT photo archive contains thousands of photographs taken by many unidentified workers and volunteers over the years. Because of the nature of CAT's undertaking and the time in which many of these photographs were taken it has been impossible to establish who took many of these photographs. We have endeavoured to correctly identify those photographs we are certain belong to someone else but please get in touch with us if we have got anything wrong and we will correct in subsequent editions.

Page 15: Educational activities at CAT (clockwise from top).

1. A university group visiting CAT, with a very simple DIY solar water heater. Leading the group (off picture) is one of CAT's engineers and lecturers, Arthur Butler.

2. Students studying on CAT's post-graduate courses take part in one of the practical activities. The courses are always a mix of practical and academic workshops and lectures.

3. Former education officer Julie Bromilow (far left) shows a group of local school children and teachers around gardener Roger McLennan's (far right) vegetable field. This sits in front of CAT's residential Eco-cabins. The field provides fresh salad for the restaurant. Many children who stay in the Eco-cabins do not know where food comes from or how it grows.

4. Education officer Christine McLennan demonstrates one of CAT's wind kits. CAT's education team have created many projects, books and classroom resources over the years, including *Where's the Impact?*, which used the ingredients, packaging and contents of a Kinder Egg to help school-aged children understand the environmental impact of everyday objects.

Page 20: Some of CAT's construction projects 1974–1992 (clockwise from top left).

1. Renovating the quarry cottages (named Cottage 1, 2 and 3 from left to right). You can see an array of solar panels on Cottage 2. Cottage 1 was later given a pitched roof with a solar space-heating device (see experimental pictures on page 111).

2. Volunteers and workers lived on site in caravans for many years. The caravans were old, cold and leaky, until someone came up with the bright idea of spraying them with insulating foam. Not now recommended as a good environmental material, the insulating foam did however serve a purpose.

3. Cindy Harris (left) and another member of the 'women's team' working on the top station of the cliff railway. This was one of CAT's most ambitious timber frame structures. The 'men's team' sadly did not totally complete their structure (the bottom station) in time for the opening, as evidenced from photographs recording the day.

4. The finished station with one of the cliff railway carriages just leaving or arriving. The top carriage is filled with water until there is enough weight to bring the bottom carriage up. Railway operator Chris Parrot's interview contains everything you need to know about the cliff railway … and more!

5. Eirig Humphries, poet and stonemason, working on CAT's restaurant and shop in the mid 1970s. You can read about Eirig on page 55.

Page 21: Some of CAT's construction projects 1997–2010 (clockwise from top left).

1. The glass roof on the Autonomous Environmental Information Centre (AtEIC), designed by Pat Borer and David Lea. Underneath the roof you can see a rammed earth wall. Heat from daytime solar gain is absorbed in the walls to keep the

temperature inside the structure more even. The heat is released from the walls when the temperature drops.

2. This same principle was scaled up when Pat and David designed the Wales Institute for Sustainable Education (WISE). Here you can see the rammed earth wall of the Sheppard lecture theatre.

3. The Gerard Morgan-Grenville courtyard is a beautiful space based on simple Japanese-influenced design ideas, but also serves to collect and move on rainwater from the main structure. Channels of water run down into the old water wheel pit (off picture to the right), which used to house a water wheel designed and built by Christopher Loudon Wallis, the son of Barnes Wallis, inventor of the bouncing bomb.

4. WISE in construction. A time lapse camera was set up to record the construction process, which, as it turned out, was a lot longer and more difficult than expected.

Page 34: The visitor centre.

1. The construction of a new lake to store water ready to be fed into the carriages of the water balanced cliff railway was part of the Gear Change project. It created a beautiful habitat for carp, ducks and other wildlife and was designed by Peter Harper.

2. Prince Philip visiting CAT in 1974. Alongside him in this photo are Gerard Morgan Grenville (far left), Mark Mathews (right) and a rather sniffy-looking unknown (far right). There wasn't much to see in 1975 so perhaps the sniffy look was understandable! There was however a steam train supposedly powered by straw pellets, which had to be helped out by some rather more traditional (carbon-emitting) coal on the day. Prince Philip allegedly discovered the coal under the straw pellets and was reported to have said "I thought so!"

Page 35: The visitor centre (clockwise from top left).

1. Farmer and engineer Edward Jones helped CAT to lift its cliff
    railway carriages into place; it's uncertain whether he appears
    in the picture. The cliff railway was CAT's most ambitious
    engineering project, overseen by CAT's engineers including
    Roger White, Clive Newman, Rob Gwillim and semi-retired civil
    engineer David Watson. It transformed the visitor experience
    and showed how water power could be used to solve a difficult
    problem.

2. An early solar power experiment to demonstrate and test the
    efficiencies of various PV modules and solar water heating panels,
    including manufactured and DIY products. CAT often pointed
    out manufacturers' claims that were 'optimistic' and through its
    information service, publications and courses has been able to
    pass on independent advice to consumers throughout its history.

3. One of the Quarry Kids in front of a map of the site. The phrase
    'Village of the Future' was used in the early days but dropped
    later on for other, perhaps more accurate, phrases: 'Europe's
    leading eco-centre' or 'living laboratory' being two. Phrase
    mythology is an important part of any institution's history, to be
    tested and critiqued. Many of CAT's early building projects were
    based on traditional vernacular architecture so the 'village of the
    future' resembled rather more 'a village from the past'.

4. CAT's gardens have been the main attraction for many visitors.
    Far from offering a manicured National Trust experience, the
    gardens emphasised experimentation and progressive organic
    horticulture over looks, but could also be very beautiful, calm and
    cosy spaces to enjoy during a visit. The picture shows the inside
    of a polytunnel. Previously containing mini-allotments for site-
    community residents, the system became difficult to maintain
    while meeting the demands of a visitor experience and instead
    was transformed into this showcase for organic production.

5. The very popular wave machine. Waves were made when the handle was moved up and down. The waves pushed round a small water turbine which generated electricity to power a small light in the light house (off picture to the right).

Page 41: Sewage treatment at CAT (clockwise from top left).

1. Former CAT biologist, current lecturer and co-author of *Lifting the Lid* Louise Halestrap (far left) with a group of ecological sewage treatment course participants 'testing' a range of manufactured compost toilets in the late 1990s. CAT tended to prefer home-made solutions (see below, as you usually could). Photo appears by kind permission of Lynn Williams.

2. Former CAT biologist and co-author of *Choosing Ecological Water Treatment and Supply* Chris Weedon shows the Eco-cabins reed beds to a group of day visitors on a guided tour. People staying in the Eco-cabins can chose between using a compost toilet or a flush toilet. If they chose to flush this is where the flush goes.

3. This is one of CAT's more salubrious conveniences, originally built for the caravans (one of which you can see in the rear of the photo). It was a 'twin-vault' toilet: one vault would be in use whilst the contents of the other turned into compost. A discreet vault door around the back could be lifted to allow for removal of the finished compost. Photo appears courtesy of Lesley Bradnam.

4. Urine is full of nitrogen, a very useful resource in any garden, but especially valuable in places where soil is in short supply. Urine at CAT was collected in 'Pee Chest', a rather ornate one-roomed building with a spire. A rudimentary funnel-based collection device was offered to the men. I'm rather ashamed to say I don't recall how the women fared.

5. Former CAT biologist and co-author of *Lifting the Lid* Peter Harper using his head for research and innovation, testing the width of a drop hole.

Page 44: The CAT site in 2006.

This photo was taken by Cristian Barnett for *The Organic Garden* (written by myself and Chloe Ward) and is published here by kind permission of Cristian and Harper Collins.

Page 52–53: The Quarry (clockwise from top left).

1. Illustrator John Urry's graphic representation of life for the early volunteers, originally drawn for a celebration of CAT's 10th anniversary. John, Graham Preston and Patrick Borer have been responsible for most of CAT's graphic output, either in publications or displays. This is typical of the wry humour CAT used to get its message across. Most of the early signs had few words, relying instead on visual interpretations.

2. Artist Glenn Davidson recording sounds in what is now CAT's disused quarry as part of his residency in 2014. This photograph is reprinted with his kind permission. Some of the original quarry works can still be seen in the quarry and are valued as important objects of industrial heritage, but can only be visited on appointment.

3. The Waites building was built in 1975 and for many years was the most energy efficient house in Britain. It is still used as a demonstration house but we have to point out that we wouldn't build a house this way again (with very thick walls and very small windows). I lived upstairs as a volunteer in the summer of 1994 and my weekend lie-ins were often interrupted by the voices of visitors, repeating "This is the most energy efficient house in Britain" as they entered.

4. Probably taken in 1973 or the first months of 1974, this picture shows the machine sheds once used for cutting slate. They were eventually transformed into offices, an exhibition hall and CAT's restaurant and first shop.

5. A group of Llwyngwern Quarry workers. We are uncertain of the provenance of this picture. It was found in a digital archive of CAT's photographs.

Page 60: The Quarry Café and Shop (clockwise from top).

1. CAT biologist Jeremy Light (far left) and Engineer Guy Watson (far right), enjoying the sunshine outside the Quarry Café in Machynlleth.

2. *Chop It, Cook It, Eat It* featured wholefood recipes used in the Quarry Café and on-site restaurant at CAT as well as a graphic representation of Quarry Café manager Annie Lowmass (as seen here on the cover).

3, 4.   The Quarry Café and Shop in the late 1970s or early 1980s.

5. Many people were intrigued but suspicious of the new vegetarian shop in the late 1970s, never quite making it over the threshold!

Page 65: The gardens at CAT (possibly in the late 70s or early 80s).

CAT's gardens at their most verdant, not bad for an old quarry! Soil had to be brought in and built up with compost made on site using plant, animal and human waste. The greenhouse contained an experimental fish farm. In the background you can see a large fishpond.

Pages 76–77: Co-operative working (clockwise from top left).

1. Picture taken on the occasion of the visit of Prince Charles in 1978. Prince Charles was invited to open CAT's forge but this picture of CAT staff and families is taken outside Tea Chest.

2. This picture was almost certainly taken in 1974 and includes Mary Mathews, CAT's first co-director. We have some other pictures from around this table which include Gerard Morgan-Grenville and Diana Brass.

3. Volunteers and staff unload CAT's first turbine in 1974, which was originally placed in the old quarry before being moved to a better position in what later became the visitor centre. Those pictured include Rod James (centre, standing) and Mark Mathews (to the left of Rod, looking).

4. Tea break with the families outside what will become the restaurant. Includes Jeremy Light (right) and Rod James (back).

5. These polystyrene panels were used as insulation in the inter-seasonal storage heater (see below), to keep the heat in. Access was and still is a problem at CAT and often lorry drivers have refused to carry their load up to the top, necessitating a great deal of physical labour. A key-stone of working life at CAT for many years was stepping out of one's normal role to help with collective tasks.

6. Resources have always been tight at CAT but there has always been a tradition of cake when someone leaves. This illustration perfectly shows the dilemma of a community that wants to be generous but must be frugal. It also says something about the notion of sharing in difficult times. The first time I came to CAT our volunteer group received a welcoming cake, which was left in Tea-Chest with a little note saying 'help yourself'.

Pages 94–95: Site community (clockwise from top left).

1. The Desirable Residence is an ironic advert probably placed on the staff noticeboard to attract a new site community resident. Rents were cheap but the accommodation was basic. I lived in Cottage 4 for a year and found it damp, dark, drafty and incredibly romantic.

2. This picture was taken in top office, the hub of CAT's office activities for many years.

3. Here one of the Quarry Kids stands on the railway line, which was built in 1970s by CAT staff to help move slate and machinery around the site. But for the children – once sitting upon a flatbed railway carriage – it was a perilous, adventure-filled fun-ride!

4. At its height the smallholding at CAT included cows, goats, chickens, geese and pigs but most people at CAT were amateurs when it came to looking after the animals. In his interview John Urry recalls many amusing and not-so amusing stories in the life of the smallholding.

5. Here you can see one of our interviewers, Irene Galant, and possibly daughter Suzanne, enjoying a picnic on one of the railway carriages. Behind the railway carriage is a DIY solar water heating panel made out of central heating radiators.

6. Roger and Christine McLennan outside their cottage with daughter Catherine and son Michael.

7. A worker outside one of the soon to be renovated cottages.

8. Site community residents Jo and Linda Gwillim featured in a national newspaper article. Such articles and headlines were common as CAT drew comparisons to 1970s sitcom *The Good Life* or in this case to the TV drama *Forever Green* (1989–1992).

9. Professional cyclist to be Yanto Barker (on the trike) in the mid 1980s, exploring the world of work from a not too safe distance. As home and work life seamlessly ran into one another, children could fully experience a wide range of communal activities and parts of adult life most children in Britain don't often see.

10. I'm not sure what's going on in this picture. This one obviously needs to be 're-storied'!

Page 106: Wind power at CAT (clockwise from top).

1. Rod James (centre) unfurling the Cretan windmill in 1974/5. Commonly used in southern European countries to generate mechanical power, this one was adapted by CAT to create a tiny amount of electrical power.

2. Jacinta MacDermot unfurling a Cretan in the 1990s. Although the Cretan has not been used at CAT for many years it was often brought out at festivals such as Glastonbury.

3. Roger White (left) shows off his Aerotron wind turbine (see page 105 for more information). Photo appears courtesy of Roger White.

Page 107: Wind power at CAT (clockwise from top left).

1. Hugh Piggott, Tim Kirby, Pete Raine (left to right) with someone I haven't been able to identify examining the ground works for the Polenko wind turbine, at the time one of the UK's largest wind turbines. Photo appears courtesy of Roger White.

2. The Polenko wind turbine being erected. Photo appears courtesy of Roger White.

3. Media officer Sarah Jenkinson, Chris Ford and unknown (left to right) standing by the blades of one of CAT's community wind farm scale turbines.

4. The Nordtank wind turbine owned by Bro Dyfi Community Renewables (BDCR) which generates electricity on the hills above CAT.

Page 110: Experiments at CAT (clockwise from top left).

1. Prince Charles, Rod James and one of CAT's many pigs. The pigs were fed kitchen scraps over the summer and slaughtered before

winter. The killing of the pig generated an annual all-staff debate, which one year included the hiring of a medium to ask the pigs what they wanted. Listen to John Urry's interview to find out what happened.

2. The chicken house. Foxes roam the site at night and many chickens have been lost over the years.

3. Constructing the base of the so-called 'Trombe' wall, which could be more accurately described as a solar collector. The collector faced a hill so a large proportion of the heat collected in it actually came from the part that formed the roof and faced the sky.

4. The polystyrene blocks (featured earlier being carried up the hill) were placed in the interseasonal storage heater. These were then covered with a waterproof liner and the heater filled with solar heated water trickling down from the office roof. Listen to the interviews of Pat Borer, Bob Todd and Rod James to find out if it worked.

5. The caravans sprayed with insulating foam, as described earlier.

6. The base of the interseasonal storage heater dug into the quarry.

7. The water wheel at CAT built by Christopher Loudon Wallis, the son of Barnes Wallis. It didn't power anything but was enjoyed by visitors.

Page 111: Experiments at CAT (clockwise from top left).

1. The finished 'Trombe' wall on Cottage 1. Trombe walls are more suited to alpine environments. It worked up to a point but was eventually removed.

2. *An Alternative Energy Strategy* was first published in 1977. You can download a copy of it from the archive website: archive.cat.org.uk Years later this became the inspiration for the Zero Carbon Britain project.

3. Another experiment with fish farming, this time outside Tea-Chest. I would love to know the story behind this picture!

4. The CAT workforce lays a lining for the fish pond.

5. Roger White (left) installing a solar tracking device

6. One of CAT's early 'how to compost' signs. CAT's compost experiments were numerous and inventive; one of them led to the creation of the high fibre composing method also known as 'cool composting', which was widely taken up by local authorities around Britain. Listen to Peter Harper's interview to find out more.

7. This photograph needs 're-storying'!

Page 115: *Zero Carbon Britain: Rethinking the Future,* launched at the Houses of Parliament.

This photograph includes (from left to right): Rebecca Sullivan, Laura Blake, Paul Allen, myself, Chris Moreton, Tobi Kellner, Alice Hooker-Stroud, Freya Stanley-Price, Ling Li, Richard Delahay, Sarah Everitt, Danni Pafford.

A brief timeline

1974   CAT opens with a £20,000 donation. First hydro installed. First school group visit. Prince Philip visits.

1975   CAT opens as a visitor centre. 5kW Elektro windmill arrives.

1976   First residential course on Alternative Technology. Quarry Association starts with 350 members.

1977   *An Alternative Energy Strategy for the UK* published. Site-wide re-build of old slate buildings. Solar panel test monitoring undertaken. Central control room opens.

1978   Prince Charles visits. First education packs published. Smallholding opens.

1979   Quarry wholefood shop opens in Machynlleth. Salad lunches start. CAT courses launched.

1980   First wind turbine for Scottish isles built by the Llwyngwern Forge Company. Buy Green Buy Mail launched.

1981   Methane digester arrives.

1982   Dulas Engineering Ltd founded at CAT.

1983   10kW wood gasification system installed.

1984   Polenko wind turbine installed.

1986   Educational magazine *Green Teacher* launched.

1988   Eco-cabins built. Aber Instruments founded at CAT. Ultra low-energy refrigerators tested and installed.

1989   Share launch to raise one million pounds. Walter Segal self build house completed.

1990 Alternative Technology Association launched.

1991 Cliff railway finished.

1992 First full year with new cliff railway sees all-time high for visitor numbers.

1995 CAT Publications launches 'New Futures' book range.

1996 Largest PV roof in UK installed.
CAT launches website: www.foe.co.uk/CAT

1997 600kW MS4 wind turbine installed.

1998 CAT creates cool composting method. *The Whole House Book* published.

1999 First BSc in Sustainable Technology launched with CAT. CAT helps first reality TV show Castaway 2000 with consultancy and training for participants.

2000 Strawbale Theatre finished. AtEIC Environmental Information Centre opened.

2001 CAT's First MSc course launched with the University of East London. AtEIC wins Gold Medal for Architecture at the National Eisteddfod.

2002 Education officers advise new Welsh Assembly. *Little Book of Slugs* sells 20,000 copies.

2003 Compost show garden at BBC Gardeners' World Live. First community wind turbine in Wales erected with CAT.

2004 Donations help CAT buy its site. WISE project launched.

2005 Carbon Gym carbon calculator goes to Glastonbury.

2006 Bringing the Future Forward project revamps the visitor circuit.

2007   Graduate School for the Environment launched. First *Zero Carbon Britain* report published.

2008   350 kW Combined Heat and Power plant installed. Professional Diploma in Architecture started.

2010   WISE opened. *Zero Carbon Britain 2030* launched. CAT's co-operative management structure replaced with hierarchy.

2012   Financial crisis leads to redundancies.

2013   CAT PLC closes. *Zero Carbon Britain: Rethinking the Future* launched. New biomass building opens.

2014   New MSc in Adaptation and Sustainability. CAT celebrates its 40th anniversary. CAT archive deposited at the National Library of Wales.

Acknowledgements

Much to my regret I haven't been able to include the oral testimonies of many of the interviewees. Every single interview I conducted was an incredible experience. One of the real pleasures for me was to sit down and share time with people, many of whom I had known for years, many I was meeting for the first time. Omission from this book does not mean that they were any the less interesting; it just means time was against me.

But I hope this book is just the start of something bigger. We want to work with our partner organisations to develop more creative opportunities to keep the archive alive, make it more available to people in many interesting ways and to recognise more fully the incredible journey CAT has taken.

The Voices from a disused quarry oral history project was funded by Glasu, the estate of Gerard Morgan-Grenville and the Society for Environmental Improvement (SEI). I would like to thank Margaret Morgan-Grenville, the SEI trustees and all the staff of Glasu for their continued support. I would also like to thank the K. Blundell Trust for supporting my work as an author.

I would like to thank Michael Pearson and Lorena Troughton at the National Library of Wales, Nathalie Camus and Iolo Williams at the Arts Council of Wales, Sarah Higgins, Sarah Vaughan, Ann MacDonald, Kerry Evans and Heike Roms of the University of Aberystwyth, Hazel Thomas and Berian Ellis at the People's Collection of Wales.

Thanks to my fellow Unearthed members for being with me throughout the project: Ariana Jordão, Rosie Leach and Claire Bracegirdle.

Thanks to Paul Allen, Peter Harper, Rebecca Sullivan and Catriona Toms for editorial comments.

A very big thank you to all the interviewers: Jess Allen, Claire Bracegirdle, Sally Carr, Gill Caves, Rebecca Edwards, Irene Galant, Peter Harper, Ariana Jordão, Rosie Leach, David Lloyd, Jane Lloyd Francis, Megan Mills, Dai Speake, Amy Staniforth, Frances Stoakley, Adrienne Thomas, Cara Walker and Calista Williams.

And all 100 interviewees, listed in the date order they were interviewed: Judith Thornton, Jill Sutherland, Judith Varley, Ann Compton, John Compton, Tom Barker, Margaret Sheppard, Geoffrey White, Janice Jackson, Katie Brown, Mark Mathews, Roderick James, Pete Raine, Roger Kelly, Angus Light, Meri Wells, Patrick Borer, Patrick Hannay, Audrey Beaumont, Don Bennett, Annie Lowmass, Chris Parrot, Paul Allen, Louise Halestrap, Elizabeth Todd, Peter Harper, Jill Whitehead, Jo Gwillim, Rennie Telford, Chloe Ward, Danny Jones, Gayle Light, Jeremy Light, Christine McLennan, Graham Preston, Roger White, Catherine McLennan, Rick Dance, Caroline Oakley, Martin Ashby, Delyth Rees, Alex Randall, Tanya Hawkes, Roger McLennan, Huw Jones, Sabrina Wise, Alison Bantham, Rachel Lilley, Andy Rowland, Clive Newman, Cindy Harris, Bob Todd, Julie Bromilow, Rob Nicklen, Julie Jones, Megan Mills, Nick Mills, Iolo Ap Gwynn, Cynog Dafis, Joan Randle, Martin Ashby, David Lea, Irene Galant, Nick Fenwick, Maureen Sedgewick, Godfrey Boyle, Maritsa Kelly, Phoebe Gauntlett, Michael Williams, Phil Horton, Nigel Dudley, Sally Carr, Jonathon Gross, Kelvin Mason, John Urry, Edward Jones, Gwilym Fychan, James Cass, Des Rees, Lesley Bradnam, Sam Harris, George Morgan-Grenville, Janet Davies, Mark Bloomfield, Jenny Gallaty, Thea Platt, Hele Oakley, Sally Oakes, Jake Voelcker, Richard Darlington, Jane Bryant, Ann MacGarry, Bethan Bennett, Lynda Wenman, Damian Randle, Gemma Light and Eileen Kinsman.

Thanks also to the Holdfast interviewees: Rachel Lilley, Kim Bryan, Sally Carr, Tanya Hawkes, Ann MacGarry and Diana Reynolds.

And the artists in residence: Anne Marie Carty, Dan Gifford, Christine Mills, Carlos Pinatti and Glenn Davidson.

Thank you to Julia Letts, Rib Davis and Rob Perks of the Oral History Society.

And last, but definitely not least, to those who have supported the project in various ways over the last three years: Lynn Williams, John Cantor, Dave Thorpe, Jonathon Porritt, Esther Tew, Cara Whelan, Joanna Wright, Paul Allen, Rebecca Sullivan, Jane Hoy, Catriona Toms, Kit Jones, Kim Bryan, Tobi Kellner, Annika Faircloth, Graham Preston, Elwyn Pugh, Tim Jenkins, Rob Nicklen,

Trish Andrews, Simon Wood, Tony Brown, Pete Telfer, Elfyn Jones and Carwyn Jones.

Finally I would just like to thank the project for taking me with it on its journey. It has been a revelation for me, and I emerge blinking from the other side of it in a completely different place to the one I occupied when I entered it. It has been one of the most fulfilling experiences of my life, and I really look forward to seeing where the experience will take me next.

About the author

Allan Shepherd is CAT's Publisher. He came to CAT for a weekend in 1994 and is now in his 21st year. As CAT Publications' marketing officer he project led two award winning educational show gardens at BBC Gardeners' World Live and successfully positioned CAT's publications in front of a mainstream audience. Since becoming Publisher in 2008 he has been responsible for publishing two editions of the *Zero Carbon Britain* report and a series of energy related titles including *Wind Power Workshop* and *The Home Energy Handbook*. He has also written nineteen books, including *The Little Book of Slugs*, *Curious Incidents in the Garden at Night-time* and *The Organic Garden*. He was organic gardening columnist for *Garden News* magazine and a finalist for The Garden Media Guild Columnist of the Year. He has also written for *The Guardian*. Since 2011 he has been the project leader for the *Voices from a disused quarry* oral history project.